BJJ Notebook

Your Brazilian Jiu-Jitsu Journey

Thadeu Vieira

ISBN: 1466322357
ISBN-13: 978-1466322356

VISIT

WWW.BJJNOTEBOOK.COM

FOR ADDITIONAL MATERIAL

CONTACT

If you find this book, please contact

_____

Name

_____

Phone

_____

Email

or

_____

Name

_____

Phone

_____

Email

CONTENTS

PREFACE

One of the easiest things in the world to do is to start training in BJJ as a beginner and then quit. This is, in fact, what happens to most people who decide to train in BJJ. Of all students that begin training in BJJ as no-stripe white belt, less than 5% will make it to black belt. A large part of this statistic is the inherently challenging nature of BJJ. But another large part is the lack of effort on the part of BJJ schools to truly cultivate beginning students. Here, cultivating beginners doesn't mean coddling or spoon feeding. It does not mean a reduction in training standards and lax discipline that have caused certain martial arts to devolve into nothing more than bizarre calisthenics. Rather, it means engaging with beginners in a manner that makes them feel welcome and part of something special. It means being attentive to their particular situation and frustrations so that they know they are not alone. It means engaging them in an ongoing discussion about BJJ as they train while providing them with the tools and instruction they need to succeed in proportion to their effort. This is common sense. It is also good business.

A beginning BJJ student cannot help having preconceived notions and high expectations about what their BJJ experience will be like. However, BJJ is unlike most other martial arts. Promotions in rank come far slower. Progress is more difficult because the training is reality based. There is no faking it. Beginning students typically train with and are constantly being dominated by more advanced students. This can be frustrating to the average student and infuriating to the student with an ego. It is easy for a beginner to feel lost on the mat and wonder why things aren't clicking.

At some point along the way, reality sets in and the high expectations and preconceived notions about what the experience was supposed to be like are shattered. This is a critical moment in a student's training because it presents a profound mental challenge. Either the student grows from the experience and moves forward or shrinks in the face of the challenge and quits.

Unfortunately, many BJJ schools don't help beginning students understand and appreciate the mental aspects of BJJ to get them beyond this wall. While every student's ultimate goal should be to master the art of BJJ, each student's journey will be different. People come to BJJ from all walks of life and over the entire spectrum of humanity. Some students are young and physically strong but mentally weak. Some students are older and not as physically strong but are more mature and mentally strong. Some are physically handicapped. Some have learning disabilities.

There is no "one-size-fits-all" BJJ. Every student will receive and internalize the lessons of BJJ in a unique way and create their own personalized version of BJJ. This one of the beautiful aspects of BJJ. Each student has the opportunity to access the infinite variety and richness of BJJ and create their own work of art that becomes part of their person. There are precious few things in life that can claim to provide such a wholesome and rewarding benefit.

To reap the full benefits of BJJ and achieve BJJ self-actualization takes a great deal of work, patience and commitment over an extended period of time. ***But there is no reason to make this job harder than it needs to be.*** One way to facilitate the BJJ growth process is for students to keep a notebook to track their progress and to record their experiences. A BJJ notebook serves the practical purpose of helping remember all of the different moves that were taught over previous weeks, months and years. In

BJJ, one can go years without seeing the same move taught twice. If a move is taught by an instructor and then quickly forgotten, how is that different from never having learned it in the first place?

Equally as important, a BJJ notebook serves as a personal journal that allows a student to break down their experiences and process them so that they can learn from them. This is an invaluable way to help connect the mental and physical aspects of BJJ. The faster a BJJ student can get the neurons in their brain configured to connect the mental with the physical and bypass the need to actually think about what moves to execute, the faster he or she will progress. This is in fact the ultimate goal of BJJ: to achieve a state of Zanshin, which is a martial arts term meaning "total awareness," and in particular the ability to react without thinking while staying relaxed.

Helio Gracie, one of the founding fathers of BJJ, said that "BJJ is for everyone." This statement should be viewed as commandment given to BJJ schools not unlike the commandments given to Moses from On High. People will try and quit BJJ for a variety of reasons beyond a BJJ school's control. However, *no one should quit BJJ because they didn't have every opportunity to succeed.*

This BJJ notebook is designed to make the most out of the beginning steps in what is hopefully a long and fruitful BJJ journey. Encouraging the use of the BJJ notebook is one of the ways a BJJ school can make the BJJ journey more accessible to those willing to put in the effort. It can serve as a basis to promote discussion and interaction among students about issues they are facing and allow students to learn from each other. The BJJ journey will still take enormous work and dedication. However, the BJJ notebook should at least provide a mechanism to help focus the student's effort to get the most of the BJJ experience.

- Xerife

INTRODUCTION

In 1995, while I was a white belt with just a couple of months of training, I heard my master, Paulo Wesley Lopes, answer a question that a student asked him. The student wanted to know how he was able to come up with an answer for every technical question and how one can reach a skill level where he could develop new moves on their own.

Master Paulo's answer:
-"What do you think? I study this at home every day!"

I thought to myself: wait a minute! How can a person train BJJ at home? We need mats, people, more people, and a teacher! Back in 1995 there was not a single VHS instruction tape of Brazilian Jiu-Jitsu. We watched the UFC by renting the video tape at the local video store! There was no YouTube, The Internet was dial-up, and smart phones were more than a decade away!

Another thing that intrigued me was the laminated piece of paper master Paulo carried with him during class. It was the requirements for a student to be able to move up from white belt to blue belt. The white belt curriculum had about 80 techniques. It sounded like way too much for a beginner. It was interesting because only he was able to decode what each term meant. For example, right on the first paragraph it said: *7th sweep*. I thought: *What does it mean? How am I going to remember 7 sweeps?*

One night after class I saw an older guy writing down in his own words how to perform the moves we learned in class. He encouraged me to do the same and I did. Every night after class from that day on I wrote down what I had learned on a sheet of paper, which I then stored under the mattress of my bed.

When I got my purple belt, I was already an assistant instructor and was proficient at the techniques of our curriculum. I remember the day that I was cleaning my room and I lifted the mattress to find over 300 pages of BJJ notes all spread out and unorganized. I read a couple of them and realized that the simple exercise of writing down what I had learned in class reinforced the lessons and allowed me to become a BJJ instructor. To my infinite regret, I threw all those papers away, never imaging they could be valuable information to me today. I guess if I had a binder or something like that, I would have kept all of that invaluable information to this day.

When training with Master Paulo, I was intrigued by the fact that he never taught a move by only saying for example: *grab it by the arm*. He was always precise when teaching, and so instead would say: *Grab on the gi behind the triceps*. He always used proper anatomical terms, which lead me to conclude that he studied the human body. He also always used terms as frontal, lateral, flexion, extension, torsion, etc. Later on he told me he has been always interested in Kinesiology. Those were some of master Paulo's secrets of seeking knowledge and studying Brazilian Jiu-Jitsu at home. It reflects his dedication and passion for the art.

I hope you embark on this journey with the same passion and determination. May this notebook help you to stay focused and motivated so you can one day become a Brazilian Jiu-Jitsu Black Belt.

1 HISTORY

Jiu-Jitsu originated over 2500 years ago. It was created by a non-threatening nomadic tribe of Buddhist monks who were frequently robbed by others. Because of their religious beliefs, they were forbidden to use any type of arms. Thus Jiu-Jitsu developed as a set of self-defense techniques based on animal movements. Jiu-Jitsu was unique in that it was developed in a manner that allowed a weak individual to overcome a much stronger individual by the judicious use of leverage. This fighting technique soon crossed Asia and reached Japan, where it became a fighting art of the Samurai.

Jiu-Jitsu in Japanese means 'gentle art'. It is a self defense style whose essence is to use as little energy as possible with maximum effect. The Buddhist monks' application of physical laws such as leverage, timing, balance, center-of-gravity, force and speed and was ahead of its time.

BRAZIL

In 1917, world Judo and Jiu-Jitsu champion Mitsuyo Maeda, known as Conde Koma, was sent to Brazil by the Japanese government on a diplomatic mission to help Japanese immigrants establish themselves in Brazil. Conde Koma first settled in Belém, in the State of Pará. He soon started teaching Jiu-Jitsu to a small group of friends.

The first member of the Gracie family to arrive in Belém was Gastão Gracie, son of James Gracie from Scotland. He established himself in Rio de Janeiro as a banker in 1870. While working for the Brazilian State Department, he traveled to Belém, where he met his wife. He soon after settled in the area, working as a businessman.

Gastão had five children: Carlos, Oswaldo, Gastão Filho, George and Hélio. Conde Koma, who had arrived in Belém in 1917, became a friend of Gastão and started teaching his oldest son, Carlos. He soon began to teach Jiu-Jitsu to Gastão's other sons.

In the late 1920's the Gracie family moved back to Rio de Janeiro. They opened the first Jiu-Jitsu school there in 1930. Hélio, a skinny and weak teenager, has been forbidden by the doctors to practice martial arts. However, he spent whole days watching his oldest brothers train in Jiu-Jitsu. He learned the fighting techniques of Jiu-Jitsu by observation.

One day, Carlos was late for the class and Hélio replaced him as the instructor. After it became clear that Hélio had an aptitude for Jiu-Jitsu, he starting training and soon was regularly instructing. After the death of Conde Koma in 1928, Carlos started to teach his other brothers everything he had learned from his master as a way to honor him and keep the martial art alive.

With a goal of proving Jiu-Jitsu's superiority over other martial arts, Carlos challenged the greatest fighters of his time. He also managed the fighting careers of his brothers. Because they were fighting and defeating opponents fifty or sixty pounds heavier, the Gracies quickly gained recognition and prestige.

The word of the achievements of the Gracie family reached Japan. In 1951, Master Matsuito Kimura, five time world champion in Judo, came to Rio to challenge Hélio. Master Kimura was accompanied by the vice-champion named Kato. When Kimura first saw Hélio, he refused to fight him as Hélio seemed so weak. He felt superior to Hélio and had Kato fight in his spot. Kato and Hélio fought in September of 1951. The fight ended tied, as Hélio had a broken rib due an early accident. In the end of the same month of September Hélio fought Kato again, but this time in São Paulo. Hélio submitted Kato on the second round, as Kato passed out by a choke.

Due the victory by Hélio over Kato, Kimura felt obligated to challenge Hélio. Kimura was 66 pounds heavier and nine years younger. Kimura decided that if his opponent lasted three minutes against him, Hélio could be declared the winner. Hélio resisted thirteen minutes. Kimura eventually won by an armlock that is known today by his name, the Kimura.

Kimura was so impressed with Hélio's technique that invited him to teach at the Imperial Academy of Japan. However, Hélio refused as he didn't want to leave his family in Brazil. The defeat at the hands of Kimura did not hurt Hélio's prestige. On the contrary, his bravery and courage during his match with Kimura transformed him into a national hero of Brazil.

2 INSIDE THE ACADEMY

The BJJ dojo, like majority of other martial arts dojos, is a place of respect and tradition. All members are expected to be cordial and respectful. With time, as you get along with colleagues and your instructor, you will become part of the pack. Jiu-Jitsu is a lifestyle. The atmosphere of a good BJJ Dojo will make it seem like a home away from home.

Always remember once you enter the mats, it is serious business. So be respectful, especially when interacting with your instructor. Even though the BJJ dojo is less formal than most martial arts dojos, do not fail to remember that that there is hierarchy and you are a student within that hierarchy. If the instructor or student of higher rank asks you to do something, there should not be a lot of discussion about why – Just do it. Be prepared to receive a nickname from higher rank students or even from the instructor directly – nicknames are part of the Brazilian culture as a form to break the ice and make one feel part of the group. As a general rule, try to follow the suggestions below:

- Never invite a higher rank student to spar with you. Traditionally, a higher rank student will invite a beginner to spar as a way to help the learning process by sharing his experiences. The other way around can be seen as a challenge.

- Never overreact or lash out after losing a match. Such acts will make you look like a target as the other students will try to teach you a lesson. Enter the mats willing to learn and to lose, knowing that losing is part of the learning process. Brazilian Jiu-Jitsu can be a truly humbling experience. There is no shame in tapping out and starting over, as long as you are giving it your best.

– Never drill less than the amount set by the instructor. If you and your partner end your drill before everybody else, do more! If you cheat on the amount of repetitions you're not cheating the instructor, you're delaying your progress.

– Pay your dues on time or ahead of time. Show support to your academy and appreciation for the knowledge that is being transferred to you. Training without paying is enormously disrespectful to the instructor

– Manage your personal hygiene to the highest standards. Wash your gi regularly—that is to say, after every time you use it in class. Make sure to trim your finger nails and toe nails so that you don't cut people or damage the mats. Do not train with open wounds. Do not be surprised if the instructors and higher rank students take you to task for hygiene infractions. Save yourself the embarrassment by being responsible.

– Once you embrace BJJ in your life, remember that the instructor was willing to accepted a disciple. He will be watching not only how you perform on the mats, but outside as well. Show support! Offer to help out the school, offer to help keep the dojo clean, offer to advertise to the academy, and offer to assist in recruiting new students. These are some of the the best ways you can show your appreciation for the opportunity to practice BJJ while also helping yourself by growing the school, meeting new people from all walks of life, and generally enjoying the BJJ experience to its fullest.

BJJ NOTEBOOK

At some point Gracie Magazine published a nice article about 100 things a BJJ student should do before reaching black belt. Here are 10 tips that will help you throughout your BJJ journey:

1) Learn to balance force and technique so that you can fight as long as you can without tiring.

2) Understand that promotions are not the only objective, but are the result of effort and learning. One whose only objective is to get promotions as fast as possible will limit their potential. It is better to focus developing technical aspects of the fight. Promotions will then come naturally.

3) Realize that deep, deep down, points and the clock do not exist, while nothing is more real than those three little taps.

4) Learn to teach. This includes knowing how to conduct an entire class, plan the warm-up for that day's specific activities, pair up the students properly and cool the students off before heading home, among other things.

5) Try to take private classes. They are vital for refining your technique and learning tricks from your teacher.

6) Study your sport's basic history. Know the Jiu-Jitsu's pioneers and what they accomplished.

7) Get your bottom game on par with your top game – or at least close to it.

8) Understand how your body works. After all, each body type adapts to Jiu-Jitsu differently. Your game should be in tune with the type of body you have.

9) Absorb whatever new technique you are taught, even if it doesn't become your specialty. It very well could be your opponent's.

10) Reflect on your mistakes.

3 CHESS OR GAMBLING?

Brazilian Jiu-Jitsu has been compared with chess. The comparison is apt. But not everyone who teaches Brazilian Jiu-Jitsu does so in a manner than makes it like chess.

There are several types of Brazilian Jiu-Jitsu schools that condition the student not play chess, but rather to gamble. The gambling athlete is the one who has a limited but very well developed arsenal of offensive techniques. This type of athlete is super-confident in the techniques he has learned and fully believes in his own potential and performance. Such an athlete is generally unconcerned about defensive techniques and their technical aspects. The athlete often relies on basic or archaic concepts or simply does not know how to defend certain moves other than by the use of strength, power and determination to escape when attacked. This athlete has a great chance of being successful as long as he or she controls the fight from the beginning.

This approach leaves little room for fighting outside of a planned scenario. However, once the scenario starts unfolding along a different line than was planned, things tend to go downhill fast. The athlete becomes frustrated and insecure. The chances of reversing a bad position are limited. The mighty warrior can be quickly vanquished when he or she relies on a game plan that does not allow for reacting to the unknown or the unexpected.

The BJJ athlete that plays "chess" is the one who has the ability to set up traps and see the ones set against him. He is the one better prepared for decision making on the fly. He is the one with sufficient knowledge to defend himself in a technical way with the use of leverage, putting himself in a position of superiority after defending an attack and reacting efficiently. The BJJ chess player is one a step ahead of his opponent. He anticipates an action and processes information faster and precisely, making correct decision during combat regardless of the situation.

The chess player and the gambler signify different styles of BJJ: one relies the mind and broad skills while the other relies on pure heart and narrowly focused skills. In beginner and intermediate levels, determination and self-confidence are important to help a BJJ student to stand out and overcome challenges when facing more technically adept opponents. However, these attributes will not help the student learn how to process information and form a solid foundation of fundamental techniques on which to build. Such a foundation is necessary to develop one's game. The ability to quickly process information and deceive the opponent are skills one needs to learn as they advance, as this is what often determines the winner in combat.

4 SELF-DEFENSE

Many people look to Brazilian Jiu-Jitsu as a means for self-defense. They have the expectation that they will be well prepared for real life-threatening situations due the effectiveness of the Brazilian Jiu-Jitsu techniques.

The usual self-defense courses based on other martial arts follow a line of memorization where a limited number of moves are considered effective in a given self-defense situation.

However, one who studies Brazilian Jiu-Jitsu is introduced to another form of training. It is note merely self-defense based. The practice of Brazilian Jiu-Jitsu as sport contributes uniquely to prepare the student's greatest asset: the mind. This is the most important piece necessary to prepare an individual to face a real life threatening situation. Without the proper mental training and conditioning, the effectiveness of the pure technical knowledge is limited.

Brazilian Jiu-Jitsu training is a constant exercise in action and reaction. A BJJ fighter needs to use his or her mind as well as moving all parts of the body in harmony with the opponent's body for all actions and reactions.

BJJ training is not based on static moves. It is not based on an aggressor who reacts in select mechanical ways. Many conventional self-defense courses establish the aggressor responses during the drills. Such courses typically lack free sparring so that the student never faces unpredictable situations. This does not train the student's mind to be facile enough to handle the unknown or the unexpected.

Skilled Brazilian Jiu-Jitsu fighters have experience based on years of sparring opponents of different sizes and skills. Consequently, they are always ready to defend themselves in any situation. They are able to quickly and unconsciously analysis a situation involving an opponent or an aggressor. This analysis includes:

– Physical and mental analysis of the opponent: Identifying and estimating weight, strength, emotional control and fighting skills of the opponent or aggressor. This identification allows the selection of the most effective techniques to handle the situation, as well the moves that can expose one to risk and consequently failure.

– Distance: Constant awareness of distance to the opponent or aggressor allows one to be a step ahead to decisions about whether to close to distance, maintain it, or increase it as according to the tactics and strategy being employed.

– Surrounded Physical Space: Automatic sense of perception of flooring, levels, height and all structure limitations that represent a danger or an advantage.

– Opponent's Vulnerability: Instantaneous analysis of possible opponent's disadvantages such as particular as anatomical features (e.g., a long neck exposes the aggressor for chokes; a thick, muscular neck render chokes problematic) and clothing (e.g., a jacket triggers all collar choke techniques).

The above analysis contributes to making key decisions in a fraction of a second.

CHESS = BRAZILIAN JIU-JITSU

In a computer chess match, the computer processes all possible moves through a process of elimination, allowing itself to choose it's play with the goal of achieving a check-mate with the least possible moves in mind. The BJJ fighter does the same. He is conditioned to analyze the most effective possibilities through the choice of hundreds of moves and the creation of situations that can lead the aggressor to make a mistake, which ultimately exposes him to a submission. The BJJ fighter is at all times looking for a window to control and submit the opponent using the least amount of energy, in the least amount of time and in the most efficient way, with a minimum margin of error, while also being aware of possible ways to counter possible opponent reactions.

To achieve the level of technical and mental development needed to master self-defense to this level takes years of training. An approach to training that focuses on promotions and trophies will usually not lead down this path. The student must focus on hours of study and dedication on the mats to gradually develop and fully understand and internalize the mental and physical aspects of BJJ needed to make the art effective in any situation.

5 TECHNICAL EVOLUTION

BJJ received a great deal of attention in recent years due its enormous success in mixed martial arts competitions. BJJ has become mandatory for fighters involved in any combat where the fight could end up on the ground and continue there. The success of BJJ in mixed martial arts competitions has much to do with how BJJ was developed and how it naturally evolves over time. This is different than most other martial arts, which a generally weighed down by "tradition" and treat new techniques as an affront to their ancestors.

The Brazilian Jiu-Jitsu techniques follow a cycle where they are invented by some, worked on and improved by others and ultimately refined and perfected (or in the end, rejected) by still others. BJJ techniques undergo a "natural selection" process: only the strongest moves survive. Any technique having fatal flaws with either need to be adapted to make them work or they are quickly vetted and disposed of.

This evolutionary cycle is alive and well today due to a mechanism that allows for different Brazilian Jiu-Jitsu schools to interact in the spirit of competition: the tournament.

The BJJ tournament is the stage where techniques are tested to prove their effectiveness. After the success of an athlete due to the use of new techniques (usually the move becomes known by the athlete's name), athletes and coaches head back to their schools and begin to study the new moves, attempting to break them down and incorporate them into their style. In parallel, when someone exposes a new move to a true master, they usually analyze the position and respond in a way to neutralize what has been shown. They then adapt it to their own reality, with several modifications if necessary.

During this process of bringing new moves inside the academy, athletes face the foundation that sustains the process of BJJ technical development: individuality. The technique that works for one might not work for another. This frustrates those who attempt to perform a specific technique without understanding its basic principles and what is physically and mentally required to execute the technique. For instance, an inflexible person might try a sweep that requires enormous flexibility and quickly found out that the move, for them, is ineffective. Yet, the same some may click with a flexible student and prove invaluable. Once again, the technique that could pose a risk to someone may be picked up by and developed others. This cycles continues on and on.

Yet, this initial frustration is what motivates professors and students to adapt techniques by observing the minutiae of the moves and making small but critical adaptations that can enable the move to be effective. A move is developed and refined based on a host of considerations, including considerations about the individual who would use it, such as their age, technical skill level, and fighting style.

The number of possible moves in BJJ is only limited by the collective mental capacity of all of the people who practice and study BJJ. As BJJ grows, the number of techniques grows exponentially as more and more people develop an increasing number of techniques, which in turn give rise to more techniques, etc. There is a synergy in BJJ where all of the individuals involved in BJJ make the art greater than the sum of its parts. The BJJ network is like a vast computer network the provides enormous processing power to develop the art. There is no limit to the creativity of the BJJ athlete that is tied into the BJJ network.

The freedom to innovate allows one to create, adapt and refine techniques. The BJJ community allows for these techniques to be tested and further developed and refined. This is what sustains the evolutionary cycle of the art.

SPORTING REGULATIONS

The Brazilian Jiu-Jitsu rules, which are designed by the IBJJF (International Brazilian Jiu-Jitsu Federation), have changed several times through the years. These changes were made with the intention of preserving the athletes' safety while making the sport as dynamic and exciting as possible. The result of such refinement is safe tournaments and excellent techniques.

Here are some quick facts in regards to rules and its technical effects in the 90's:

- Sweeps from the half-guard were very limited, in fact the position was addressed as half-mount, as the focus and superiority was on the top player.

- Guard players were allowed to pull the opponent to his guard once the athlete was already inside the opponent's guard. Today, it is awarded two points as a sweep, which makes the athlete try to pass the guard.

- Body slams were allowed as a way to open the guard (!)

- Foot locks and leg locks were not permitted

The reason foot locks and leg locks were banned was there was the perception (mostly on the part of the spectators) that such moves were "unfair." Before the Pan-American Championship in 1996, these moves were reintroduces. Interestingly, the fighters from Brazilian were caught off guard (no pun intended) by the updated   rules that were mainly created to satisfy American competitors. And here is an interesting fact: Since in Brazil *armbar* is called *armlock*, most of the Brazilian fighters refer to the *leglock* technique as *armlock of the leg*.

Technical restrictions in competitions continue to be refined. For example, biceps locks are now allowed only for brown and black belts. Techniques such as neck cranks and pressure locks are not allowed in children divisions.

Points in the form of "advantages" were created as a way to take allow for properly scoring a close match to avoid ties. . It has been shown to be a generally fair way to award victory to the athlete who attacks more during a combat. On the other hand, the use of advantages created the somewhat conservative strategy of fighting and managing the match that relies on scoring advantages.

SAME NAME, DIFFERENT PERFORMANCE

Through this analysis, it is possible to understand why Brazilian Jiu-Jitsu schools teach techniques that have the same name but are executed differently. For example, an armbar from the guard that is taught in an academy in the Copacabana may not executed that in another academy in Ipanema. Both academies teach Brazilian Jiu-Jitsu based on different perspectives based on the origin of the schools and the technical level of their masters. The best way to prove the effectiveness of a technique is at tournaments or in an actual self-defense situation.

However, when it comes to competition, it is necessary to consider the the athlete as an individual. A well-conditioned fighter may overcome an opponent due his physical or mental superiority during combat, even when not performing every move perfectly. The opponent who did not train specific defenses may need to tap out. On the other hand, a very well-performed technique can demonstrate proof of the fundamental tenet of Brazilian Jiu-Jitsu: that the weak can overcome the strong through the use of efficient technique and leverage.

It is also important to mention that there are a great number of unqualified "instructors" leading classes in BJJ academies. Such instructors develop techniques of low quality because they do not have the talent and knowledge necessary to effectively refine techniques. Most of the time in such cases, strength rather than technique becomes the basis for the move. The technique only works for the strong. If a technique does not work for the weak, as far as BJJ is concerned, it is an illusion. It may work for a few, but that is not the point. A true BJJ technique should be almost universally applicable with appropriate modifications that account for the differences among individual BJJ students. all.

THE INTERNET

The availability of numerous videos on the Internet today demonstrates in a scary way the technical improvement process. It is too recent to conclude if the benefit will outweigh the detriment As previously mentioned, the place to prove the effectiveness of certain techniques is mainly in tournaments, and in particular those tournaments where athletes having a high level of skill are present. Moves are primarily tested first on a training partner, then with others inside the academy, then later in small tournaments and finally at big tournaments.

It is important to keep in mind that this process can send the athlete down a twisted path that can temporarily impede the learning process. A simple consult with a BJ professor or master one way to avoid such detours.

It is also important to point out that most of the techniques that an athlete believes they are developing on their own in truth are known in various forms elsewhere. This is still a useful exercise, since inventing a technique on one's own and later finding out that the move already exists serves to validate the student's thought process and direction.

6 A STRONG FOUNDATION

BJJ is an infinite network of techniques ranging from the simple to the complex. However, all of the techniques rely on BJJ fundamentals. BJJ fundamentals are invaluable to the learning process and the execution of every kind of move. Without sound fundamentals, advanced moves cannot be executed properly and will be a source of frustration instead of accomplishment.

The fundamentals include the following:

- The ground locomotion techniques;
- The 90° angle arm locks;
- The arm bars;
- The mechanics of chokes via asphyxiation;
- The mechanics of chokes via bloodstream blockage;
- The guard, mount, lateral positions (immobilization) and all fours position;
- The mechanics of submission defenses and position escapes.

The older a beginning Brazilian Jiu-Jitsu student is, the greater the importance that such student be introduced gradually to these fundamentals. We commonly tell adult beginners that the last time that they were adapted to the ground for locomotion was when they were crawling as a baby. Once we take our first steps, we never have the same contact with the floor and lose the acquired skills of locomotion in the horizontal position. This requires new students to get re-introduced to ground movement and ground positions.

Fundamental BJJ submissions appear simple but are actually quite complex. The same is true with ground locomotion and ground positions. Although they all look simple when performed by an experience BJJ student, it tends to be a great deal harder than it looks. Thus, it is critical that the student's execution of BJJ fundamentals reach a high level of accuracy and precision.

THE INSTRUCTOR'S RESPONSIBILITY

Many BJJ instructors make the mistake of introducing a beginner student to too many advanced techniques too soon. While it is natural for students to be curious about advanced moves, this curiosity needs to be held in check with the help of the BJJ instructor. Likewise, the BJJ instructor needs to not get caught up in demonstrating advanced techniques just to demonstrate his superior his knowledge.

Skipping the natural process of learning techniques gradually and to a set curriculum commensurate with a student's ability compromises the learning process and is detrimental to the student's long-term progress. Once the student who skips steps reaches a higher rank, he will not have the skill set necessary to face an opponent who has a proper BJJ foundation. He will not have had the opportunity to break techniques down and study their origins, variations and forms of neutralization. He will more than likely end up being an incomplete fighter with limited ability to process information on the fly and deal with the unexpected.

The athlete that is trained correctly and without skipping learning steps develops the habit of processing and analyzing unknown situations in an unlimited way. Such an athlete is able to develop new positions and is able to neutralize possible attacks that were unknown during a combat.

MIXED MARTIAL ARTS

During the Mixed Martial Arts (MMA) fights in the 1990's, the fighters' predominant styles were based on standing techniques. Once on the ground, they were easy prey for BJJ fighters. Not only for the submission capability that BJJ represented, but also due the lack of knowledge of basic ground moves. These fighters were viewed as incomplete. They were like a "fish out of water" once they hit the ground.

Today in MMA we see the majority of fighters training BJJ. That doesn't make them great submission and ground masters. However, it proved that having a basic knowledge of ground techniques provided the ability to effectively defend themselves on the ground while also employing their respective martial arts style and strategy when standing.

Unfortunately, with the near universal acceptance of BJJ for the "ground game" in MMA, many Brazilian Jiu-Jitsu Pro MMA fighters have been tempted to switch their strategy to rely on stand-up skills such as boxing skills. This has proven to be a mistake for fighters and and improvement for other fighters. It is well accepted that MMA fighters who face an authentic BJJ black belt avoid going to the ground at all costs. It can be very frustrating for BJJ fans to see their representative spending time playing a standing game. The taste of the victory is definitely not the same – grappling fans want to see the "Tap Out".

7 MOTOR SKILLS

BJJ requires the use of a remarkably high number of motor skills to accomplish a great variety of different movements and physical actions. These include walking, jumping, crawling, crouching, rolling in every direction, grabbing, sitting, laying, standing, throwing, falling, spinning, pushing, pulling. It also requires engaging all of a person's limbs and in some cases the head. BJJ can be incredibly acrobatic even though it takes place ostensibly on the ground.

All the above mentioned movements and physical actions can happen in all directions - forward, backward, lateral, diagonal, top and bottom, right-side up as well as upside-down. This makes BJJ one of the most complex sports.

Is very important that the necessary physical abilities and motor skills mentioned above be gradually developed by beginners during the learning process. This is accomplished by practicing and mastering the BJJ fundamentals such as shrimping, rolling, standing up properly, proper posture in the guard, etc.

My observation from years of teaching BJJ and observing beginning students is when a BJJ student has difficulty learning and executing a BJJ technique, the underlying reason can usually be traced to some shortcoming in their learning and incorporating one or more of the fundamentals

LEFT OR RIGHT

During the practice of new techniques, many students become confused as to the manner a movement must be executed: due motor skills or coordination deficiencies. It is interesting to see that some students avoid the practice of movements to both sides, while others are actually intrigued to try it.

During the learning process of a new position, the brain adjusts in order to process the information and memorize it, allowing later on the integration between consciousness and the execution of such movement when sparring. This is a crucial moment for the learning process. It is advised that the student experience the technique with enough time and encouragement. Learning the move from one side at first will help to build the necessary confidence in their motor skills, so later on the student can perform the same move on the other side. Otherwise, physical rejection will be generated, which will be translated as mental rejection of the technique. This is when the student tells himself that he does not like the move, and he will not incorporate it into his game.

MANY PATHS

Eventually, making mistakes during the learning process of a movement might cause the athlete to discover new possibilities. It is important to have an accurate critical sense about everything that is experienced in the dojo, in order to constantly develop the perception field.

The performance of the armbar from the guard for example; by a beginner, when taught in the most basic form using a foot on the hip as a pivot point for the hip escape – when the movement of the hips is done to the "wrong" side, the athlete would execute the technique on the arm where there is no fulcrum in the application of a lever. The elbow joint would be turned upwards without any contact with the groin area. However, based on the mistaken positioning of the athlete's body, new possibilities arise. In similar situations, the continuation of the movement of an omoplata (shoulder lock) with the legs can be applied, which works with a triangle choke as well.

The intent to deceive the opponent's attention in regards to an attack must be studied carefully.

In practice or even in competition, the ability for an effective decision is a matter of perception, reasoning, and reaction time. Such abilities can be developed in technical and tactical training at advanced levels. The athlete can put himself in an uncomfortable position or an unexpected one, and naturally having to react in the most efficient possible form, respecting his individual skill at that moment.

8 RANK ADVANCEMENT

To this date, there is not a pre set form of evaluation or standards to advance one in rank in Brazilian Jiu-Jitsu, except after the black belt, which degrees are awarded by the Federations only according to the set of rules established by the IBJJF. Generally, from white to black belt, an instructor can advance the rank of his students by any means he deems necessary.

In the face of so many benefits brought up by the BJJ craze, an ambitious race for the black belt is happening everywhere. The goal for such status is moved sometimes by ego, vanity, or possible financial advantages. Unfortunately, this creates weakness in the BJJ community.

A good portion of instructors are responsible for allowing the traditional links between master and disciple to be lost in time. Academies that have the sole objective of obtaining results in tournaments, and not so much in the formation of the individual give margin to the student, which generally does not create a sense of loyalty. Loyalty is something that has been interwoven in martial arts tradition, since the beginning of time. Students are seduced by other unethical academies that promise a faster rank advancement and other benefits.

The student should always trust in his master and have humility to accept the current rank the master believes is appropriate at that time.

Those who do not have a consistent lineage and a relationship with a genuine master throughout the years are suspects of having achieved the black belt status in "windy ways."

BELT TEST

Nowadays, numerous academies advance rank uniquely based on tournament performance, and for those who do not compete they have to wait until the instructor decides the day has come without any qualitative or quantitative basis. Either way, does not fit the technical-didactic structure that is involved in Brazilian Jiu-Jitsu. A lot of instructors out there do not know the true meaning of the color belts, which is to identify the amount of knowledge one has and not solely to identify who beats who. Why not quantify this knowledge in evaluations or test? Many academies that teach authentic Brazilian Jiu-Jitsu still resist the external pressure created by teams that do not have such standards, but have a bigger reach towards the new adepts of BJJ, and maintain the old-fashion belt test in their curriculum.

The BJJ learning process must be introduced as a form of study and technical domain. When the student is ready to advance in rank, the belt test is a great tool to create an opportunity where the practitioner and the instructor can present to the families and community the results of hard work in the form of wisdom.

9 BODY & MIND

A lot of people quit or do not even start Brazilian Jiu-Jitsu classes because the misconception in regards to the fitness level necessary to take such classes. Let one thing to be clear; nobody is already in shape for BJJ unless you do BJJ or some similar activity. You can bring a swimmer, a weight lifter or even a marathon runner, and they will not last more than a couple minutes in a match, condition-wise. BJJ is one of the most physically demanding activities that exists. The athlete literally uses their entire body at all times. The energetic system used in BJJ is predominantly anaerobic, therefore the ordinary person who is not an athlete is not conditioned for such activity. The problem is that a lot of people get discouraged by this fact, when they should just understand that all the other people that are training right now began at the same point!

The secret is to increase your time on the mats, but not for increasing strength or resistance, but to learn how to not waste one's energy. You will only compensate the unnecessary use of force when you acquire technical knowledge and get to implement it when sparring.

FLOW DRILL

There is an amazing form of exercise that will condition a student to understand Brazilian Jiu-Jitsu in its essence: the flow drill. This training system helps with movement, timing, breathing, and numerous other things. In BJJ, the major benefit of the flow drill is to teach students how to move in order to better understand their body mechanics. The drill helps one in understanding how to move their own body, as well as understanding how their partner's body moves. It is not about strength or speed. It is more about about utilizing proper techniques and movements. It is a cooperative effort between you and your partner. When you feel your partner is throwing you off-balance, you go with the flow. When you throw your partner off-balance and sweep or reverse him, he goes with the flow. While performing at this pace, without forcing a position, neither you nor your partner will be able to apply a submission. You can momentarily establish the hold, but there is no application. You simply transition out of it and continue on with the drill.

This is a fantastic way to teach students how to not use their strength. As it is with many new students a huge obstacle for them to overcome. It also helps you to understand how to regulate your breathing. It ultimately teaches you how to think through various positions.

10 SEMINAR ATTENDANCES

It is very common among BJJ academies to host clinics and seminars with various black belts. Keep an eye open for when other academies nearby you advertise about a special guest as you might have the chance to train with a BJJ star and even with a Gracie legend.

Seminars are a great way to experience different techniques and teaching skills. There is always something good to take out of a seminar. Usually, BJJ seminars range from two to four hours in a very informal atmosphere and sense of camaraderie.

During a seminar, a student is bombarded by dozens of techniques. Even though you perform several repetitions, it is very common for you to get to the end of a seminar barely remembering the first moves you learned just a couple of hours prior. Use the following pages to describe techniques or tips that caught your attention, so you can go back to your academy and practice without forgetting them.

Date:_____/_____/_____   Location:_____

Instructor:_____

TECHNIQUES & HIGHLIGHTS

_____
_____
_____
_____
_____
_____
_____
_____
_____
_____
_____
_____
_____
_____
_____
_____
_____
_____
_____
_____
_____
_____
_____
_____
_____

COMMENTS

_____
_____
_____
_____
_____

PHOTO

OF THIS

SEMINAR

BJJ NOTEBOOK

Date:____/____/____   Location: _____

Instructor:_____

TECHNIQUES & HIGHLIGHTS

_____
_____
_____
_____
_____
_____
_____
_____
_____
_____
_____
_____
_____
_____
_____
_____
_____
_____
_____
_____
_____
_____
_____

COMMENTS

_____
_____
_____
_____
_____

PHOTO

OF THIS

SEMINAR

Date:____/____/____   Location:_____

Instructor:_____

TECHNIQUES & HIGHLIGHTS

_____
_____
_____
_____
_____
_____
_____
_____
_____
_____
_____
_____
_____
_____
_____
_____
_____
_____
_____
_____
_____
_____

COMMENTS

_____
_____
_____
_____

PHOTO

OF THIS

SEMINAR

BJJ NOTEBOOK

Date:____/____/____   Location:_____

Instructor:_____

TECHNIQUES & HIGHLIGHTS

_____
_____
_____
_____
_____
_____
_____
_____
_____
_____
_____
_____
_____
_____
_____
_____
_____
_____
_____
_____
_____
_____
_____
_____
_____

COMMENTS

_____
_____
_____
_____
_____

PHOTO

OF THIS

SEMINAR

Date:____/____/____   Location:_____

Instructor:_____

TECHNIQUES & HIGHLIGHTS

_____
_____
_____
_____
_____
_____
_____
_____
_____
_____
_____
_____
_____
_____
_____
_____
_____
_____
_____
_____
_____
_____
_____

COMMENTS

_____
_____
_____
_____
_____

PHOTO

OF THIS

SEMINAR

Date:____/____/____   Location:_____

Instructor:_____

TECHNIQUES & HIGHLIGHTS

_____
_____
_____
_____
_____
_____
_____
_____
_____
_____
_____
_____
_____
_____
_____
_____
_____
_____
_____
_____
_____
_____
_____

COMMENTS

_____
_____
_____
_____
_____

PHOTO

OF THIS

SEMINAR

11 WEIGHT TRACK

CHECK YOUR WEIGHT BY-WEEKLY

Date: 9 / 9 / 15   Weight: 185lb 84ᵏᵍ ( ) Gi (✓) No-Gi
Date: ___/___/___   Weight: _____ ( ) Gi ( ) No-Gi
Date: ___/___/___   Weight: _____ ( ) Gi ( ) No-Gi
Date: ___/___/___   Weight: _____ ( ) Gi ( ) No-Gi
Date: ___/___/___   Weight: _____ ( ) Gi ( ) No-Gi
Date: ___/___/___   Weight: _____ ( ) Gi ( ) No-Gi
Date: ___/___/___   Weight: _____ ( ) Gi ( ) No-Gi
Date: ___/___/___   Weight: _____ ( ) Gi ( ) No-Gi
Date: ___/___/___   Weight: _____ ( ) Gi ( ) No-Gi
Date: ___/___/___   Weight: _____ ( ) Gi ( ) No-Gi
Date: ___/___/___   Weight: _____ ( ) Gi ( ) No-Gi
Date: ___/___/___   Weight: _____ ( ) Gi ( ) No-Gi
Date: ___/___/___   Weight: _____ ( ) Gi ( ) No-Gi
Date: ___/___/___   Weight: _____ ( ) Gi ( ) No-Gi
Date: ___/___/___   Weight: _____ ( ) Gi ( ) No-Gi
Date: ___/___/___   Weight: _____ ( ) Gi ( ) No-Gi
Date: ___/___/___   Weight: _____ ( ) Gi ( ) No-Gi
Date: ___/___/___   Weight: _____ ( ) Gi ( ) No-Gi
Date: ___/___/___   Weight: _____ ( ) Gi ( ) No-Gi
Date: ___/___/___   Weight: _____ ( ) Gi ( ) No-Gi
Date: ___/___/___   Weight: _____ ( ) Gi ( ) No-Gi
Date: ___/___/___   Weight: _____ ( ) Gi ( ) No-Gi
Date: ___/___/___   Weight: _____ ( ) Gi ( ) No-Gi
Date: ___/___/___   Weight: _____ ( ) Gi ( ) No-Gi
Date: ___/___/___   Weight: _____ ( ) Gi ( ) No-Gi
Date: ___/___/___   Weight: _____ ( ) Gi ( ) No-Gi
Date: ___/___/___   Weight: _____ ( ) Gi ( ) No-Gi
Date: ___/___/___   Weight: _____ ( ) Gi ( ) No-Gi
Date: ___/___/___   Weight: _____ ( ) Gi ( ) No-Gi

12 YOUR BJJ JOURNEY

The time has come for you to write down your own history. The idea behind this notebook is to aid you in learning from your own past. Fill-in each page of this book with as much detail as possible. Every word will become a powerful tool toward a big step in the right direction.

This notebook will benefit both the ordinary BJJ student that trains a few times a week, and also the student who has competition as a major goal. The last chapter will allow you to keep records of your matches in order to generate important statistics for further analysis. Those students who do not wish to participate in tournaments can use the records section of the book for mock tournaments or internal events at their academy.

In the middle of the book, you will find common questions about Jiu-Jitsu, the Gracie family, and several exercises.

BJJ NOTEBOOK

Date: ___ / ___ / ___

What techniques did you learn today?

_____

_____

_____

_____

_____

Describe important technical details or tips you learned today:

_____

_____

_____

_____

_____

_____

_____

_____

_____

_____

Sparring comments:

_____

_____

_____

_____

What do you need to improve at this point?

_____

_____

_____

_____

Notes:

_____

_____

_____

_____

What techniques did you learn today?

Date: ____/____/____

_____

_____

_____

_____

_____

Describe important technical details or tips you learned today:

_____

_____

_____

_____

_____

_____

_____

_____

Sparring comments:

_____

_____

_____

_____

What do you need to improve at this point?

_____

_____

_____

_____

Notes:

_____

_____

_____

_____

BJJ NOTEBOOK

Date: _____ / _____ / _____

What techniques did you learn today?

_____
_____
_____
_____
_____

Describe important technical details or tips you learned today:

_____
_____
_____
_____
_____
_____
_____
_____
_____

Sparring comments:

_____
_____
_____
_____

What do you need to improve at this point?

_____
_____
_____

Notes:

_____
_____
_____

Date: ___ / ___ / ___

What techniques did you learn today?

_____
_____
_____
_____
_____

Describe important technical details or tips you learned today:

_____
_____
_____
_____
_____
_____
_____
_____
_____

Sparring comments:

_____
_____
_____
_____

What do you need to improve at this point?

_____
_____
_____

Notes:

_____
_____
_____
_____

BJJ NOTEBOOK

Date: ____ / ____ / ____

What techniques did you learn today?

_____

_____

_____

_____

_____

Describe important technical details or tips you learned today:

_____

_____

_____

_____

_____

_____

_____

_____

_____

Sparring comments:

_____

_____

_____

_____

_____

What do you need to improve at this point?

_____

_____

_____

_____

Notes:

_____

_____

_____

_____

Date: ____ / ____ / ____

What techniques did you learn today?

_____
_____
_____
_____
_____

Describe important technical details or tips you learned today:

_____
_____
_____
_____
_____
_____
_____
_____
_____

Sparring comments:

_____
_____
_____
_____

What do you need to improve at this point?

_____
_____
_____

Notes:

_____
_____
_____

BJJ NOTEBOOK

Date: _____ / _____ / _____

What techniques did you learn today?

_____

_____

_____

_____

_____

Describe important technical details or tips you learned today:

_____

_____

_____

_____

_____

_____

_____

_____

_____

Sparring comments:

_____

_____

_____

_____

What do you need to improve at this point?

_____

_____

_____

_____

Notes:

_____

_____

_____

_____

Date: ___/___/___

What techniques did you learn today?

_____
_____
_____
_____
_____

Describe important technical details or tips you learned today:

_____
_____
_____
_____
_____
_____
_____
_____
_____

Sparring comments:

_____
_____
_____
_____

What do you need to improve at this point?

_____
_____
_____

Notes:

_____
_____
_____
_____

BJJ NOTEBOOK

Date: _____ / _____ / _____

What techniques did you learn today?

_____
_____
_____
_____
_____

Describe important technical details or tips you learned today:

_____
_____
_____
_____
_____
_____
_____
_____
_____

Sparring comments:

_____
_____
_____
_____

What do you need to improve at this point?

_____
_____
_____
_____

Notes:

_____
_____
_____
_____

Date: ___/___/___

What techniques did you learn today?

_____
_____
_____
_____
_____

Describe important technical details or tips you learned today:

_____
_____
_____
_____
_____
_____
_____
_____
_____

Sparring comments:

_____
_____
_____
_____

What do you need to improve at this point?

_____
_____
_____

Notes:

_____
_____
_____

BJJ NOTEBOOK
QUESTION & ANSWER

Q) What is the full name of your instructor?

A) _____

Q) What is your instructor's lineage?

A) _____
_____
_____

Q) What is the order of the belts in BJJ?

A) _____
_____
_____

Q) How are the Rank Advancement criteria in your school?

A) _____
_____
_____

Q) What are the names of the five Gracie brothers?

A) _____
_____
_____

Q) Who is the current instructor of your instructor and where does he live?

A) _____
_____
_____
_____
_____

Date: ___ / ___ / ___

What techniques did you learn today?

_____

_____

_____

_____

_____

Describe important technical details or tips you learned today:

_____

_____

_____

_____

_____

_____

_____

_____

_____

Sparring comments:

_____

_____

_____

_____

What do you need to improve at this point?

_____

_____

_____

_____

Notes:

_____

_____

_____

_____

BJJ NOTEBOOK

Date: ____ / ____ / ____

What techniques did you learn today?

_____

_____

_____

_____

_____

Describe important technical details or tips you learned today:

_____

_____

_____

_____

_____

_____

_____

_____

_____

Sparring comments:

_____

_____

_____

_____

What do you need to improve at this point?

_____

_____

_____

Notes:

_____

_____

_____

Date: ___ / ___ / ___

What techniques did you learn today?

_____
_____
_____
_____
_____

Describe important technical details or tips you learned today:

_____
_____
_____
_____
_____
_____
_____
_____
_____

Sparring comments:

_____
_____
_____
_____

What do you need to improve at this point?

_____
_____
_____
_____

Notes:

_____
_____
_____
_____

BJJ NOTEBOOK

Date: _____ / _____ / _____

What techniques did you learn today?

_____
_____
_____
_____
_____

Describe important technical details or tips you learned today:

_____
_____
_____
_____
_____
_____
_____
_____
_____

Sparring comments:

_____
_____
_____
_____

What do you need to improve at this point?

_____
_____
_____
_____

Notes:

_____
_____
_____
_____

Date: ____ / ____ / ____

What techniques did you learn today?

_____

_____

_____

_____

_____

Describe important technical details or tips you learned today:

_____

_____

_____

_____

_____

_____

_____

_____

_____

Sparring comments:

_____

_____

_____

_____

What do you need to improve at this point?

_____

_____

_____

Notes:

_____

_____

_____

BJJ NOTEBOOK
TECHNICAL DESCRIPTION

Describe in your own words and in maximum detail, as if you were teaching a new student in your academy, how to perform a perfect armbar from the mounted position.

_____
_____
_____
_____
_____
_____
_____
_____
_____
_____
_____
_____
_____
_____
_____
_____
_____
_____
_____
_____
_____
_____
_____
_____
_____
_____
_____
_____
_____
_____

Date: ____ / ____ / ____

What techniques did you learn today?

_____

_____

_____

_____

_____

Describe important technical details or tips you learned today:

_____

_____

_____

_____

_____

_____

_____

_____

_____

Sparring comments:

_____

_____

_____

_____

What do you need to improve at this point?

_____

_____

_____

_____

Notes:

_____

_____

_____

_____

Date: ____ / ____ / ____

What techniques did you learn today?

_____
_____
_____
_____
_____

Describe important technical details or tips you learned today:

_____
_____
_____
_____
_____
_____
_____
_____
_____

Sparring comments:

_____
_____
_____
_____

What do you need to improve at this point?

_____
_____
_____

Notes:

_____
_____
_____
_____

Date: ___ / ___ / ___

What techniques did you learn today?

_____
_____
_____
_____
_____

Describe important technical details or tips you learned today:

_____
_____
_____
_____
_____
_____
_____
_____
_____

Sparring comments:

_____
_____
_____
_____

What do you need to improve at this point?

_____
_____
_____

Notes:

_____
_____
_____

BJJ NOTEBOOK

Date: _____ / _____ / _____

What techniques did you learn today?

_____
_____
_____
_____
_____

Describe important technical details or tips you learned today:

_____
_____
_____
_____
_____
_____
_____
_____
_____

Sparring comments:

_____
_____
_____
_____

What do you need to improve at this point?

_____
_____
_____

Notes:

_____
_____
_____

THE GUARD
BASIC POSITIONS

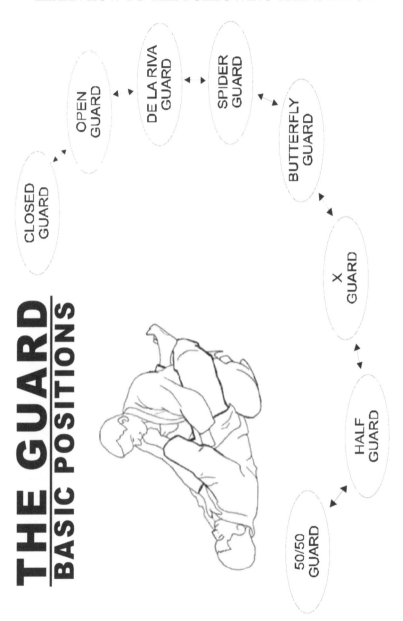

CLOSED GUARD

OPEN GUARD

DE LA RIVA GUARD

SPIDER GUARD

BUTTERFLY GUARD

X GUARD

HALF GUARD

50/50 GUARD

BJJ NOTEBOOK

Date: ____ / ____ / ____

What techniques did you learn today?

_____

_____

_____

_____

_____

Describe important technical details or tips you learned today:

_____

_____

_____

_____

_____

_____

_____

_____

_____

Sparring comments:

_____

_____

_____

_____

What do you need to improve at this point?

_____

_____

_____

Notes:

_____

_____

_____

INSTRUCTOR FEEDBACK
(To be completed by your instructor only)

Progress notes:

_____

_____

_____

_____

_____

_____

_____

_____

_____

_____

Strengths *(Best qualities, techniques, etc)*:

_____

_____

_____

_____

_____

Needs to improve:

_____

_____

_____

_____

Target techniques:

_____

_____

_____

_____

BJJ NOTEBOOK

Date: ____ / ____ / ____

What techniques did you learn today?

_____

_____

_____

_____

_____

Describe important technical details or tips you learned today:

_____

_____

_____

_____

_____

_____

_____

_____

_____

_____

Sparring comments:

_____

_____

_____

_____

What do you need to improve at this point?

_____

_____

_____

_____

Notes:

_____

_____

_____

_____

Date: ___/___/___

What techniques did you learn today?

_____
_____
_____
_____
_____

Describe important technical details or tips you learned today:

_____
_____
_____
_____
_____
_____
_____
_____
_____

Sparring comments:

_____
_____
_____
_____

What do you need to improve at this point?

_____
_____
_____
_____

Notes:

_____
_____
_____
_____

BJJ NOTEBOOK

Date: ___ / ___ / ___

What techniques did you learn today?

_____

_____

_____

_____

_____

Describe important technical details or tips you learned today:

_____

_____

_____

_____

_____

_____

_____

_____

_____

_____

Sparring comments:

_____

_____

_____

_____

What do you need to improve at this point?

_____

_____

_____

_____

Notes:

_____

_____

_____

_____

What techniques did you learn today?

Date: ____ / ____ / ____

_____

_____

_____

_____

_____

Describe important technical details or tips you learned today:

_____

_____

_____

_____

_____

_____

_____

_____

_____

Sparring comments:

_____

_____

_____

_____

What do you need to improve at this point?

_____

_____

_____

_____

Notes:

_____

_____

_____

_____

BJJ NOTEBOOK

Date: ____ / ____ / ____

What techniques did you learn today?

_____

_____

_____

_____

Describe important technical details or tips you learned today:

_____

_____

_____

_____

_____

_____

_____

_____

Sparring comments:

_____

_____

_____

What do you need to improve at this point?

_____

_____

_____

Notes:

_____

_____

_____

QUESTION & ANSWER

Q) What is the best BJJ Magazine or BJJ website in your opinion?

A) _____

CONNECT THE COLUMNS CORRECTLY

How many points do you score if you perform the following?

Front mount ·	· 3
Knee on the belly ·	· 0
Escape from the mount ·	· 4
Passing the guard ·	· 4
Sweeps ·	· 0
Back grab ·	· 0
Escape from side control ·	· 2
Take down ·	· 4
Back mount ·	· 2
Defending an armbar ·	· 2

Q) Who is your favorite Gracie family member?

A) _____

Q) Who is the current highest rank in BJJ still alive?

A) _____

Q) Which UFCs (Ultimate Fighting Championship) did Royce Gracie beat?

A) _____
_____
_____
_____

Date: ____ / ____ / ____

What techniques did you learn today?

_____

_____

_____

_____

_____

Describe important technical details or tips you learned today:

_____

_____

_____

_____

_____

_____

_____

_____

_____

Sparring comments:

_____

_____

_____

_____

What do you need to improve at this point?

_____

_____

_____

Notes:

_____

_____

_____

What techniques did you learn today?

_____
_____
_____
_____
_____

Describe important technical details or tips you learned today:

_____
_____
_____
_____
_____
_____
_____
_____
_____

Sparring comments:

_____
_____
_____
_____

What do you need to improve at this point?

_____
_____
_____

Notes:

_____
_____
_____

BJJ NOTEBOOK

Date: _____ / _____ / _____

What techniques did you learn today?

_____
_____
_____
_____
_____

Describe important technical details or tips you learned today:

_____
_____
_____
_____
_____
_____
_____
_____
_____

Sparring comments:

_____
_____
_____
_____

What do you need to improve at this point?

_____
_____
_____
_____

Notes:

_____
_____
_____
_____

Date: ____ / ____ / ____

What techniques did you learn today?

_____

_____

_____

_____

_____

Describe important technical details or tips you learned today:

_____

_____

_____

_____

_____

_____

_____

_____

_____

Sparring comments:

_____

_____

_____

_____

What do you need to improve at this point?

_____

_____

_____

_____

Notes:

_____

_____

_____

_____

BJJ NOTEBOOK

Date: ____ / ____ / ____

What techniques did you learn today?

_____
_____
_____
_____
_____

Describe important technical details or tips you learned today:

_____
_____
_____
_____
_____
_____
_____
_____
_____

Sparring comments:

_____
_____
_____
_____

What do you need to improve at this point?

_____
_____
_____

Notes:

_____
_____
_____

What techniques did you learn today?

_____

_____

_____

_____

_____

Describe important technical details or tips you learned today:

_____

_____

_____

_____

_____

_____

_____

_____

_____

Sparring comments:

_____

_____

_____

_____

What do you need to improve at this point?

_____

_____

_____

_____

Notes:

_____

_____

_____

_____

BJJ NOTEBOOK

Date: _____ / _____ / _____

What techniques did you learn today?

_____
_____
_____
_____
_____

Describe important technical details or tips you learned today:

_____
_____
_____
_____
_____
_____
_____
_____
_____

Sparring comments:

_____
_____
_____
_____

What do you need to improve at this point?

_____
_____
_____
_____

Notes:

_____
_____
_____
_____

Date: ___ / ___ / ___

What techniques did you learn today?

_____
_____
_____
_____
_____

Describe important technical details or tips you learned today:

_____
_____
_____
_____
_____
_____
_____
_____
_____

Sparring comments:

_____
_____
_____
_____

What do you need to improve at this point?

_____
_____
_____

Notes:

_____
_____
_____
_____

BJJ NOTEBOOK

Date: _____/_____/_____

What techniques did you learn today?

_____

_____

_____

_____

_____

Describe important technical details or tips you learned today:

_____

_____

_____

_____

_____

_____

_____

_____

_____

Sparring comments:

_____

_____

_____

_____

What do you need to improve at this point?

_____

_____

_____

_____

Notes:

_____

_____

_____

_____

TECHNICAL DESCRIPTION

Describe in your own words and in maximum detail, as if you were teaching a new student in your academy, how to perform an escape from the mounted position.

_____

_____

_____

_____

_____

_____

_____

_____

_____

_____

_____

_____

_____

_____

_____

_____

_____

_____

_____

_____

_____

_____

_____

_____

_____

_____

_____

_____

_____

_____

BJJ NOTEBOOK

Date: ____ / ____ / ____

What techniques did you learn today?

_____

_____

_____

_____

_____

Describe important technical details or tips you learned today:

_____

_____

_____

_____

_____

_____

_____

_____

_____

Sparring comments:

_____

_____

_____

_____

What do you need to improve at this point?

_____

_____

_____

_____

Notes:

_____

_____

_____

_____

Date: ____/____/____

What techniques did you learn today?

_____
_____
_____
_____
_____

Describe important technical details or tips you learned today:

_____
_____
_____
_____
_____
_____
_____
_____
_____
_____

Sparring comments:

_____
_____
_____
_____
_____

What do you need to improve at this point?

_____
_____
_____
_____

Notes:

_____
_____
_____
_____

BJJ NOTEBOOK

Date: ____ / ____ / ____

What techniques did you learn today?

_____

_____

_____

_____

_____

Describe important technical details or tips you learned today:

_____

_____

_____

_____

_____

_____

_____

_____

Sparring comments:

_____

_____

_____

_____

What do you need to improve at this point?

_____

_____

_____

Notes:

_____

_____

_____

Date: ___ / ___ / ___

What techniques did you learn today?

_____
_____
_____
_____
_____

Describe important technical details or tips you learned today:

_____
_____
_____
_____
_____
_____
_____
_____
_____

Sparring comments:

_____
_____
_____
_____

What do you need to improve at this point?

_____
_____
_____
_____

Notes:

_____
_____
_____
_____

Date: _____/_____/_____

What techniques did you learn today?

_____
_____
_____
_____
_____

Describe important technical details or tips you learned today:

_____
_____
_____
_____
_____
_____
_____
_____
_____
_____

Sparring comments:

_____
_____
_____
_____
_____

What do you need to improve at this point?

_____
_____
_____

Notes:

_____
_____
_____

Date: ____/____/____

What techniques did you learn today?

_____

_____

_____

_____

_____

Describe important technical details or tips you learned today:

_____

_____

_____

_____

_____

_____

_____

_____

_____

Sparring comments:

_____

_____

_____

_____

What do you need to improve at this point?

_____

_____

_____

Notes:

_____

_____

_____

Date: ____/____/____

INSTRUCTOR FEEDBACK
(To be completed by your instructor only)

Progress notes:

_____

_____

_____

_____

_____

_____

_____

_____

_____

_____

Strengths *(Best qualities, techniques, etc)*:

_____

_____

_____

_____

_____

Needs to improve:

_____

_____

_____

_____

Target techniques:

_____

_____

_____

_____

What techniques did you learn today?

Date: ___ / ___ / ___

_____

_____

_____

_____

_____

Describe important technical details or tips you learned today:

_____

_____

_____

_____

_____

_____

_____

_____

_____

Sparring comments:

_____

_____

_____

_____

What do you need to improve at this point?

_____

_____

_____

_____

Notes:

_____

_____

_____

_____

BJJ NOTEBOOK

Date: _____ / _____ / _____

What techniques did you learn today?

_____

_____

_____

_____

_____

Describe important technical details or tips you learned today:

_____

_____

_____

_____

_____

_____

_____

_____

Sparring comments:

_____

_____

_____

_____

What do you need to improve at this point?

_____

_____

_____

Notes:

_____

_____

_____

What techniques did you learn today?

_____

_____

_____

_____

_____

Describe important technical details or tips you learned today:

_____

_____

_____

_____

_____

_____

_____

_____

_____

Sparring comments:

_____

_____

_____

_____

What do you need to improve at this point?

_____

_____

_____

_____

Notes:

_____

_____

_____

_____

BJJ NOTEBOOK

Date: _____ / _____ / _____

What techniques did you learn today?

_____

_____

_____

_____

_____

Describe important technical details or tips you learned today:

_____

_____

_____

_____

_____

_____

_____

_____

_____

Sparring comments:

_____

_____

_____

_____

What do you need to improve at this point?

_____

_____

_____

_____

Notes:

_____

_____

_____

_____

Date: ____/____/____

What techniques did you learn today?

_____
_____
_____
_____
_____

Describe important technical details or tips you learned today:

_____
_____
_____
_____
_____
_____
_____
_____
_____

Sparring comments:

_____
_____
_____
_____
_____

What do you need to improve at this point?

_____
_____
_____
_____

Notes:

_____
_____
_____
_____

FLOW DIAGRAM – Write on the lines techniques that are possible to be executed according to the following positions:

2 Sweeps, 4 attacks from guard and 4 attacks from mount

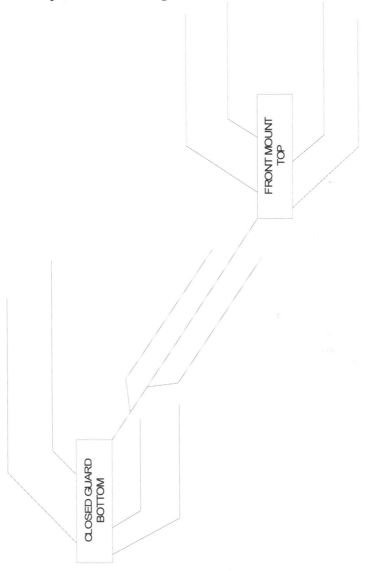

FRONT MOUNT
TOP

CLOSED GUARD
BOTTOM

Date: ____/____/____

What techniques did you learn today?

_____

_____

_____

_____

_____

Describe important technical details or tips you learned today:

_____

_____

_____

_____

_____

_____

_____

_____

_____

Sparring comments:

_____

_____

_____

_____

What do you need to improve at this point?

_____

_____

_____

Notes:

_____

_____

_____

BJJ NOTEBOOK

Date: ____/____/____

What techniques did you learn today?

_____

_____

_____

_____

_____

Describe important technical details or tips you learned today:

_____

_____

_____

_____

_____

_____

_____

_____

_____

Sparring comments:

_____

_____

_____

_____

What do you need to improve at this point?

_____

_____

_____

_____

Notes:

_____

_____

_____

_____

Date: ____ / ____ / ____

What techniques did you learn today?

_____

_____

_____

_____

_____

Describe important technical details or tips you learned today:

_____

_____

_____

_____

_____

_____

_____

_____

_____

Sparring comments:

_____

_____

_____

_____

What do you need to improve at this point?

_____

_____

_____

_____

Notes:

_____

_____

_____

_____

BJJ NOTEBOOK

Date: _____ / _____ / _____

What techniques did you learn today?

_____

_____

_____

_____

_____

Describe important technical details or tips you learned today:

_____

_____

_____

_____

_____

_____

_____

_____

_____

Sparring comments:

_____

_____

_____

_____

What do you need to improve at this point?

_____

_____

_____

Notes:

_____

_____

_____

Date: ____ / ____ / ____

What techniques did you learn today?

_____
_____
_____
_____
_____

Describe important technical details or tips you learned today:

_____
_____
_____
_____
_____
_____
_____
_____
_____

Sparring comments:

_____
_____
_____
_____

What do you need to improve at this point?

_____
_____
_____
_____

Notes:

_____
_____
_____
_____

BJJ NOTEBOOK

Date: _____ / _____ / _____

What techniques did you learn today?

_____
_____
_____
_____
_____

Describe important technical details or tips you learned today:

_____
_____
_____
_____
_____
_____
_____
_____
_____

Sparring comments:

_____
_____
_____
_____

What do you need to improve at this point?

_____
_____
_____

Notes:

_____
_____
_____

Date: ____/____/____

What techniques did you learn today?

_____
_____
_____
_____
_____

Describe important technical details or tips you learned today:

_____
_____
_____
_____
_____
_____
_____
_____
_____

Sparring comments:

_____
_____
_____
_____

What do you need to improve at this point?

_____
_____
_____

Notes:

_____
_____
_____

BJJ NOTEBOOK

Date: _____ / _____ / _____

What techniques did you learn today?

_____

_____

_____

_____

_____

Describe important technical details or tips you learned today:

_____

_____

_____

_____

_____

_____

_____

_____

_____

Sparring comments:

_____

_____

_____

_____

What do you need to improve at this point?

_____

_____

_____

_____

Notes:

_____

_____

_____

_____

What techniques did you learn today?

_____

_____

_____

_____

_____

Describe important technical details or tips you learned today:

_____

_____

_____

_____

_____

_____

_____

_____

_____

Sparring comments:

_____

_____

_____

_____

What do you need to improve at this point?

_____

_____

_____

_____

Notes:

_____

_____

_____

_____

BJJ NOTEBOOK

Date: ____ / ____ / ____

What techniques did you learn today?

_____
_____
_____
_____
_____

Describe important technical details or tips you learned today:

_____
_____
_____
_____
_____
_____
_____
_____
_____

Sparring comments:

_____
_____
_____
_____

What do you need to improve at this point?

_____
_____
_____
_____

Notes:

_____
_____
_____
_____

Date: ____ / ____ / ____

What techniques did you learn today?

_____

_____

_____

_____

_____

Describe important technical details or tips you learned today:

_____

_____

_____

_____

_____

_____

_____

_____

_____

Sparring comments:

_____

_____

_____

_____

What do you need to improve at this point?

_____

_____

_____

Notes:

_____

_____

_____

TECHNICAL DESCRIPTION

Describe in your own words and in maximum detail, as if you were teaching a new student in your academy, how to perform a Kimura from the North-South position.

_____

_____

_____

_____

_____

_____

_____

_____

_____

_____

_____

_____

_____

_____

_____

_____

_____

_____

_____

_____

_____

_____

_____

_____

_____

_____

_____

_____

_____

_____

_____

_____

Date: ____/____/____

What techniques did you learn today?

_____
_____
_____
_____
_____

Describe important technical details or tips you learned today:

_____
_____
_____
_____
_____
_____
_____
_____
_____

Sparring comments:

_____
_____
_____
_____

What do you need to improve at this point?

_____
_____
_____

Notes:

_____
_____
_____
_____

BJJ NOTEBOOK

Date: _____ / _____ / _____

What techniques did you learn today?

_____

_____

_____

_____

_____

Describe important technical details or tips you learned today:

_____

_____

_____

_____

_____

_____

_____

_____

Sparring comments:

_____

_____

_____

_____

What do you need to improve at this point?

_____

_____

_____

Notes:

_____

_____

_____

Date: ____/____/____

What techniques did you learn today?

_____
_____
_____
_____
_____

Describe important technical details or tips you learned today:

_____
_____
_____
_____
_____
_____
_____
_____
_____

Sparring comments:

_____
_____
_____
_____

What do you need to improve at this point?

_____
_____
_____

Notes:

_____
_____
_____

Date: ___/___/___

What techniques did you learn today?

_____

_____

_____

_____

_____

Describe important technical details or tips you learned today:

_____

_____

_____

_____

_____

_____

_____

_____

_____

Sparring comments:

_____

_____

_____

_____

What do you need to improve at this point?

_____

_____

_____

Notes:

_____

_____

_____

Date: ___ / ___ / ___

INSTRUCTOR FEEDBACK
(To be completed by your instructor only)

Progress notes:

_____

_____

_____

_____

_____

_____

_____

_____

_____

Strengths *(Best qualities, techniques, etc)*:

_____

_____

_____

_____

_____

Needs to improve:

_____

_____

_____

_____

Target techniques:

_____

_____

_____

_____

BJJ NOTEBOOK

Date: _____ / _____ / _____

What techniques did you learn today?

_____

_____

_____

_____

_____

Describe important technical details or tips you learned today:

_____

_____

_____

_____

_____

_____

_____

_____

_____

Sparring comments:

_____

_____

_____

_____

What do you need to improve at this point?

_____

_____

_____

_____

Notes:

_____

_____

_____

_____

Date: ____/____/____

What techniques did you learn today?

_____
_____
_____
_____
_____

Describe important technical details or tips you learned today:

_____
_____
_____
_____
_____
_____
_____
_____
_____
_____

Sparring comments:

_____
_____
_____
_____

What do you need to improve at this point?

_____
_____
_____
_____

Notes:

_____
_____
_____
_____

Date: ____ / ____ / ____

What techniques did you learn today?

_____

_____

_____

_____

_____

Describe important technical details or tips you learned today:

_____

_____

_____

_____

_____

_____

_____

_____

Sparring comments:

_____

_____

_____

_____

What do you need to improve at this point?

_____

_____

_____

Notes:

_____

_____

_____

Date: ____ / ____ / ____

What techniques did you learn today?

_____

_____

_____

_____

_____

Describe important technical details or tips you learned today:

_____

_____

_____

_____

_____

_____

_____

_____

_____

_____

Sparring comments:

_____

_____

_____

_____

What do you need to improve at this point?

_____

_____

_____

Notes:

_____

_____

_____

_____

BJJ NOTEBOOK

Date: ____/____/____

What techniques did you learn today?

_____

_____

_____

_____

_____

Describe important technical details or tips you learned today:

_____

_____

_____

_____

_____

_____

_____

_____

_____

Sparring comments:

_____

_____

_____

_____

_____

What do you need to improve at this point?

_____

_____

_____

_____

Notes:

_____

_____

_____

_____

Date: ____ / ____ / ____

What techniques did you learn today?

_____

_____

_____

_____

_____

Describe important technical details or tips you learned today:

_____

_____

_____

_____

_____

_____

_____

_____

_____

_____

Sparring comments:

_____

_____

_____

_____

What do you need to improve at this point?

_____

_____

_____

Notes:

_____

_____

_____

FLOW DIAGRAM – Write on the lines techniques that are possible to be executed according to the following positions:

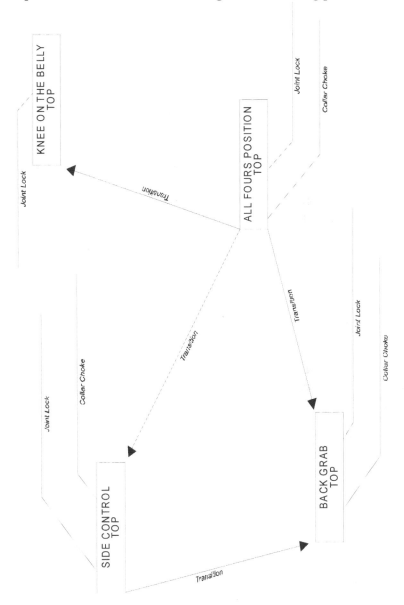

What techniques did you learn today?

Date: _____ / _____ / _____

_____
_____
_____
_____
_____

Describe important technical details or tips you learned today:

_____
_____
_____
_____
_____
_____
_____
_____
_____

Sparring comments:

_____
_____
_____
_____

What do you need to improve at this point?

_____
_____
_____

Notes:

_____
_____
_____
_____

BJJ NOTEBOOK

Date: _____ / _____ / _____

What techniques did you learn today?

_____

_____

_____

_____

_____

Describe important technical details or tips you learned today:

_____

_____

_____

_____

_____

_____

_____

_____

Sparring comments:

_____

_____

_____

_____

What do you need to improve at this point?

_____

_____

_____

Notes:

_____

_____

_____

Date: _____ / _____ / _____

What techniques did you learn today?

_____

_____

_____

_____

_____

Describe important technical details or tips you learned today:

_____

_____

_____

_____

_____

_____

_____

_____

_____

Sparring comments:

_____

_____

_____

_____

What do you need to improve at this point?

_____

_____

_____

Notes:

_____

_____

_____

BJJ NOTEBOOK

Date: _____ / _____ / _____

What techniques did you learn today?

_____
_____
_____
_____
_____

Describe important technical details or tips you learned today:

_____
_____
_____
_____
_____
_____
_____
_____
_____

Sparring comments:

_____
_____
_____
_____

What do you need to improve at this point?

_____
_____
_____

Notes:

_____
_____
_____

Date: _____ / _____ / _____

What techniques did you learn today?

_____
_____
_____
_____
_____

Describe important technical details or tips you learned today:

_____
_____
_____
_____
_____
_____
_____
_____
_____
_____

Sparring comments:

_____
_____
_____
_____

What do you need to improve at this point?

_____
_____
_____

Notes:

_____
_____
_____
_____

Date: _____ / _____ / _____

What techniques did you learn today?

_____

_____

_____

_____

_____

Describe important technical details or tips you learned today:

_____

_____

_____

_____

_____

_____

_____

_____

_____

Sparring comments:

_____

_____

_____

_____

What do you need to improve at this point?

_____

_____

_____

_____

Notes:

_____

_____

_____

_____

Date: ____/____/____

What techniques did you learn today?

_____

_____

_____

_____

_____

Describe important technical details or tips you learned today:

_____

_____

_____

_____

_____

_____

_____

_____

_____

_____

Sparring comments:

_____

_____

_____

_____

What do you need to improve at this point?

_____

_____

_____

_____

Notes:

_____

_____

_____

_____

Date: ____/____/____

What techniques did you learn today?

_____

_____

_____

_____

_____

Describe important technical details or tips you learned today:

_____

_____

_____

_____

_____

_____

_____

_____

_____

Sparring comments:

_____

_____

_____

_____

What do you need to improve at this point?

_____

_____

_____

Notes:

_____

_____

_____

What techniques did you learn today?

_____

_____

_____

_____

_____

Describe important technical details or tips you learned today:

_____

_____

_____

_____

_____

_____

_____

_____

_____

_____

Sparring comments:

_____

_____

_____

_____

What do you need to improve at this point?

_____

_____

_____

Notes:

_____

_____

_____

_____

BJJ NOTEBOOK

Date: ____/____/____

What techniques did you learn today?

_____

_____

_____

_____

_____

Describe important technical details or tips you learned today:

_____

_____

_____

_____

_____

_____

_____

_____

_____

Sparring comments:

_____

_____

_____

_____

What do you need to improve at this point?

_____

_____

_____

_____

Notes:

_____

_____

_____

_____

Date: ____/____/____

What techniques did you learn today?

_____
_____
_____
_____
_____

Describe important technical details or tips you learned today:

_____
_____
_____
_____
_____
_____
_____
_____
_____

Sparring comments:

_____
_____
_____
_____

What do you need to improve at this point?

_____
_____
_____

Notes:

_____
_____
_____

BJJ NOTEBOOK
TECHNICAL DESCRIPTION

Describe in your own words and in maximum detail, as if you were teaching a new student in your academy, how to perform an escape from the triangle choke.

Date: ___/___/___

What techniques did you learn today?

_____
_____
_____
_____
_____

Describe important technical details or tips you learned today:

_____
_____
_____
_____
_____
_____
_____
_____
_____
_____

Sparring comments:

_____
_____
_____
_____

What do you need to improve at this point?

_____
_____
_____
_____

Notes:

_____
_____
_____
_____

BJJ NOTEBOOK

Date: ____/____/____

What techniques did you learn today?

_____
_____
_____
_____
_____

Describe important technical details or tips you learned today:

_____
_____
_____
_____
_____
_____
_____
_____
_____

Sparring comments:

_____
_____
_____
_____

What do you need to improve at this point?

_____
_____
_____

Notes:

_____
_____
_____

Date: ____ / ____ / ____

What techniques did you learn today?

_____

_____

_____

_____

_____

Describe important technical details or tips you learned today:

_____

_____

_____

_____

_____

_____

_____

_____

_____

_____

Sparring comments:

_____

_____

_____

_____

What do you need to improve at this point?

_____

_____

_____

Notes:

_____

_____

_____

Date: ____ / ____ / ____

INSTRUCTOR FEEDBACK
(To be completed by your instructor only)

Progress notes:

_____

_____

_____

_____

_____

_____

_____

_____

_____

Strengths *(Best qualities, techniques, etc)*:

_____

_____

_____

_____

_____

Needs to improve:

_____

_____

_____

_____

Target techniques:

_____

_____

_____

_____

What techniques did you learn today?

Date: ____/____/____

_____

_____

_____

_____

_____

Describe important technical details or tips you learned today:

_____

_____

_____

_____

_____

_____

_____

_____

_____

Sparring comments:

_____

_____

_____

_____

What do you need to improve at this point?

_____

_____

_____

Notes:

_____

_____

_____

_____

BJJ NOTEBOOK

Date: ____ / ____ / ____

What techniques did you learn today?

_____
_____
_____
_____
_____

Describe important technical details or tips you learned today:

_____
_____
_____
_____
_____
_____
_____
_____
_____

Sparring comments:

_____
_____
_____
_____
_____

What do you need to improve at this point?

_____
_____
_____
_____

Notes:

_____
_____
_____
_____

Date: ____/____/____

What techniques did you learn today?

_____

_____

_____

_____

_____

Describe important technical details or tips you learned today:

_____

_____

_____

_____

_____

_____

_____

_____

_____

Sparring comments:

_____

_____

_____

_____

What do you need to improve at this point?

_____

_____

_____

Notes:

_____

_____

_____

BJJ NOTEBOOK

Date: ____/____/____

What techniques did you learn today?

_____

_____

_____

_____

_____

Describe important technical details or tips you learned today:

_____

_____

_____

_____

_____

_____

_____

_____

_____

Sparring comments:

_____

_____

_____

_____

What do you need to improve at this point?

_____

_____

_____

Notes:

_____

_____

_____

Date: ____/____/____

What techniques did you learn today?

_____
_____
_____
_____
_____

Describe important technical details or tips you learned today:

_____
_____
_____
_____
_____
_____
_____
_____
_____
_____

Sparring comments:

_____
_____
_____
_____

What do you need to improve at this point?

_____
_____
_____
_____

Notes:

_____
_____
_____
_____

BJJ NOTEBOOK

Date: ____ / ____ / ____

What techniques did you learn today?

_____

_____

_____

_____

_____

Describe important technical details or tips you learned today:

_____

_____

_____

_____

_____

_____

_____

_____

_____

Sparring comments:

_____

_____

_____

_____

What do you need to improve at this point?

_____

_____

_____

_____

Notes:

_____

_____

_____

_____

Date: ____ / ____ / ____

What techniques did you learn today?

_____
_____
_____
_____
_____

Describe important technical details or tips you learned today:

_____
_____
_____
_____
_____
_____
_____
_____
_____
_____

Sparring comments:

_____
_____
_____
_____

What do you need to improve at this point?

_____
_____
_____

Notes:

_____
_____
_____
_____

CREATE A LESSON PLAN

If your instructor asked you to lead a 60 minute class one day for a group of youths during his absence, how would you plan your class? How much time would you give to each section and what would you teach?

[____] minutes – STRETCHING

[____] minutes – WARM UP (Calisthenics Exercises, Rolls...)

[____] minutes – DRILL #1: _____

[____] minutes – DRILL #2: _____

[____] minutes – TECHNIQUE #1: _____

_____

_____

[____] minutes – TECHNIQUE #2: _____

_____

_____

[____] minutes – SPARRING (How many rounds? ____)

Teaching is a real art. We don't see our instructors carrying a lesson plan on a piece of paper every class, nor clocking every single activity during practice, but rest assured that instructors has a plan in their mind the minute they start a class and with experience they acquire the class management skill necessary to conduct organized classes and more important: classes that make sense to the students.

This time your instructor asked you to lead a 45 minute class for a group of kids which age group range from 4 to 6 years old. How would you plan your class?

[____] minutes – STRETCHING

[____] minutes – WARM UP/GAME #1: _____

_____

[____] minutes – DRILL/GAME #2: _____

_____

[____] minutes – TECHNIQUE #1: _____

_____

_____

[____] minutes – TECHNIQUE #2: _____

_____

_____

[____] minutes – SPARRING (How many rounds? _____)

Make sure to check the current IBJJF rules package for the technical restrictions according to each age group to make sure you don't select illegal techniques for your lesson plan.

BJJ NOTEBOOK

Date: ____/____/____

What techniques did you learn today?

_____

_____

_____

_____

_____

Describe important technical details or tips you learned today:

_____

_____

_____

_____

_____

_____

_____

_____

_____

Sparring comments:

_____

_____

_____

_____

What do you need to improve at this point?

_____

_____

_____

_____

Notes:

_____

_____

_____

_____

Date: ____/____/____

What techniques did you learn today?

_____
_____
_____
_____
_____

Describe important technical details or tips you learned today:

_____
_____
_____
_____
_____
_____
_____
_____
_____

Sparring comments:

_____
_____
_____
_____

What do you need to improve at this point?

_____
_____
_____

Notes:

_____
_____
_____
_____

BJJ NOTEBOOK

Date: ____ / ____ / ____

What techniques did you learn today?

_____

_____

_____

_____

_____

Describe important technical details or tips you learned today:

_____

_____

_____

_____

_____

_____

_____

_____

_____

Sparring comments:

_____

_____

_____

_____

What do you need to improve at this point?

_____

_____

_____

Notes:

_____

_____

_____

What techniques did you learn today?

_____

_____

_____

_____

_____

Describe important technical details or tips you learned today:

_____

_____

_____

_____

_____

_____

_____

_____

_____

Sparring comments:

_____

_____

_____

_____

What do you need to improve at this point?

_____

_____

_____

_____

Notes:

_____

_____

_____

_____

BJJ NOTEBOOK

Date: ___ / ___ / ___

What techniques did you learn today?

_____
_____
_____
_____
_____

Describe important technical details or tips you learned today:

_____
_____
_____
_____
_____
_____
_____
_____
_____

Sparring comments:

_____
_____
_____
_____
_____

What do you need to improve at this point?

_____
_____
_____
_____

Notes:

_____
_____
_____
_____

Date: ____ / ____ / ____

What techniques did you learn today?

_____

_____

_____

_____

_____

Describe important technical details or tips you learned today:

_____

_____

_____

_____

_____

_____

_____

_____

_____

Sparring comments:

_____

_____

_____

_____

What do you need to improve at this point?

_____

_____

_____

Notes:

_____

_____

_____

_____

BJJ NOTEBOOK

Date: ____/____/____

What techniques did you learn today?

_____

_____

_____

_____

_____

Describe important technical details or tips you learned today:

_____

_____

_____

_____

_____

_____

_____

_____

_____

Sparring comments:

_____

_____

_____

_____

What do you need to improve at this point?

_____

_____

_____

Notes:

_____

_____

_____

_____

Date: ____ / ____ / ____

What techniques did you learn today?

_____

_____

_____

_____

_____

Describe important technical details or tips you learned today:

_____

_____

_____

_____

_____

_____

_____

_____

_____

Sparring comments:

_____

_____

_____

_____

What do you need to improve at this point?

_____

_____

_____

_____

Notes:

_____

_____

_____

_____

BJJ NOTEBOOK

Date: ___ / ___ / ___

What techniques did you learn today?

_____

_____

_____

_____

_____

Describe important technical details or tips you learned today:

_____

_____

_____

_____

_____

_____

_____

_____

_____

Sparring comments:

_____

_____

_____

_____

What do you need to improve at this point?

_____

_____

_____

Notes:

_____

_____

_____

What techniques did you learn today?

Date: ____/____/____

_____
_____
_____
_____
_____

Describe important technical details or tips you learned today:

_____
_____
_____
_____
_____
_____
_____
_____
_____
_____

Sparring comments:

_____
_____
_____
_____

What do you need to improve at this point?

_____
_____
_____
_____

Notes:

_____
_____
_____
_____

Date: ___ / ___ / ___

What techniques did you learn today?

_____

_____

_____

_____

_____

Describe important technical details or tips you learned today:

_____

_____

_____

_____

_____

_____

_____

_____

_____

Sparring comments:

_____

_____

_____

_____

What do you need to improve at this point?

_____

_____

_____

Notes:

_____

_____

_____

What techniques did you learn today?

Date: ____/____/____

_____

_____

_____

_____

Describe important technical details or tips you learned today:

_____

_____

_____

_____

_____

_____

_____

Sparring comments:

_____

_____

_____

What do you need to improve at this point?

_____

_____

_____

Notes:

_____

_____

_____

BJJ NOTEBOOK

Date: ____ / ____ / ____

What techniques did you learn today?

_____

_____

_____

_____

_____

Describe important technical details or tips you learned today:

_____

_____

_____

_____

_____

_____

_____

_____

Sparring comments:

_____

_____

_____

_____

What do you need to improve at this point?

_____

_____

_____

Notes:

_____

_____

_____

Date: ____/____/____

What techniques did you learn today?

_____
_____
_____
_____
_____

Describe important technical details or tips you learned today:

_____
_____
_____
_____
_____
_____
_____
_____
_____
_____

Sparring comments:

_____
_____
_____
_____

What do you need to improve at this point?

_____
_____
_____
_____

Notes:

_____
_____
_____
_____

Date: ___ / ___ / ___

INSTRUCTOR FEEDBACK
(To be completed by your instructor only)

Progress notes:

_____

_____

_____

_____

_____

_____

_____

_____

_____

Strengths *(Best qualities, techniques, etc)*:

_____

_____

_____

_____

_____

Needs to improve:

_____

_____

_____

_____

Target techniques:

_____

_____

_____

_____

14 RECORDS AND STATISTICS

The only way to find out what you need to improve is to analyze your performance. Keeping records and statistics in martial arts is neglected and hard to implement by tournament organizers and federations. The most efficient way to do so is doing it individually. Thus, the responsibility of keeping data is on the athlete.

The later you start collecting performance data, the bigger the loss will be on important information. In BJJ, the average number of matches an athlete has to go through to obtain first place in an official tournament is four matches. If you compete in 3 tournaments in only a couple months, you would have to fight on average somewhere between 3 to 12 matches. That is valuable information right there, especially in terms of analyzing how opponents are scoring points or submitting you. Those are key factors that can direct your training in a way that allows you to target corrections that need to be made. It also points out effective maneuvers that can be quantified in the form of specialized moves that you know or have been working for you in a positive way.

An ordinary BJJ athlete that participates in tournaments regularly usually competes once every other month. In six months, this athlete may have fought over 20 fights. Imagine after two or three years? You can give yourself accurate feedback as long as you dedicate few minutes to keeping your records after each fight. If you need to, ask a family member or training partner to help. Understand your bracket, clock the time of each match, make notes about your performance, your weight, your diet, etc.

BJJ NOTEBOOK

Tournament:_____ Date:___/___/___

City:_____ State:____ Number of Opponents:____

Age:_____ Rank:_____ Weight:_____

Result:_____ ( ) Gi ( ) No-Gi

MATCH #1

( ) Win ( ) Loss   Final Time:_____

( ) Submission - _____

Points   **Advantages**

You [____] x [____]   You [____] x [____]

NOTES: _____

_____

_____

_____

MATCH #2

( ) Win ( ) Loss   Final Time:_____

( ) Submission - _____

Points   **Advantages**

You [____] x [____]   You [____] x [____]

NOTES: _____

_____

_____

_____

MATCH #3

( ) Win ( ) Loss   Final Time:_____

( ) Submission - _____

Points   **Advantages**

You [____] x [____]   You [____] x [____]

NOTES: _____

_____

_____

_____

MATCH #4

( ) Win ( ) Loss   Final Time:_____
( ) Submission - _____
                Points   **Advantages**
        You [____] x [____]   You [____] x [____]

NOTES: _____
_____
_____
_____

MATCH #5

( ) Win ( ) Loss   Final Time:_____
( ) Submission - _____
                Points   **Advantages**
        You [____] x [____]   You [____] x [____]

NOTES: _____
_____
_____
_____

MATCH #6

( ) Win ( ) Loss   Final Time:_____
( ) Submission - _____
                Points   **Advantages**
        You [____] x [____]   You [____] x [____]

NOTES: _____
_____
_____
_____

BJJ NOTEBOOK

Tournament:_____ Date:____/____/____
City:_____ State:_____ Number of Opponents:_____
Age:_____ Rank:_____ Weight:_____
Result:_____ ( ) Gi ( ) No-Gi

MATCH #1

( ) Win ( ) Loss   Final Time:_____
( ) Submission - _____

Points	**Advantages**
You [_____] x [_____]	You [_____] x [_____]

NOTES: _____
_____
_____
_____

MATCH #2

( ) Win ( ) Loss   Final Time:_____
( ) Submission - _____

Points	**Advantages**
You [_____] x [_____]	You [_____] x [_____]

NOTES: _____
_____
_____
_____

MATCH #3

( ) Win ( ) Loss   Final Time:_____
( ) Submission - _____

Points	**Advantages**
You [_____] x [_____]	You [_____] x [_____]

NOTES: _____
_____
_____
_____

MATCH #4

( ) Win ( ) Loss   Final Time:_____
( ) Submission - _____

| **Points** | **Advantages** |
| You [____] x [____] | You [____] x [____] |

NOTES: _____

_____

_____

_____

MATCH #5

( ) Win ( ) Loss   Final Time:_____
( ) Submission - _____

| **Points** | **Advantages** |
| You [____] x [____] | You [____] x [____] |

NOTES: _____

_____

_____

_____

MATCH #6

( ) Win ( ) Loss   Final Time:_____
( ) Submission - _____

| **Points** | **Advantages** |
| You [____] x [____] | You [____] x [____] |

NOTES: _____

_____

_____

_____

Tournament:_____ Date:____/____/____
City:_____ State:____ Number of Opponents:_____
Age:_____ Rank:_____ Weight:_____
Result:_____ ( ) Gi ( ) No-Gi

MATCH #1
( ) Win ( ) Loss   Final Time:_____
( ) Submission - _____
                 Points   **Advantages**
        You [____] x [____]   You [____] x [____]

NOTES: _____
_____
_____
_____

MATCH #2
( ) Win ( ) Loss   Final Time:_____
( ) Submission - _____
                 Points   **Advantages**
        You [____] x [____]   You [____] x [____]

NOTES: _____
_____
_____
_____

MATCH #3
( ) Win ( ) Loss   Final Time:_____
( ) Submission - _____
                 Points   **Advantages**
        You [____] x [____]   You [____] x [____]

NOTES: _____
_____
_____
_____

MATCH #4

( ) Win ( ) Loss   Final Time:_____
( ) Submission - _____

Points	Advantages
You [____] x [____]	You [____] x [____]

NOTES: _____

_____

_____

_____

MATCH #5

( ) Win ( ) Loss   Final Time:_____
( ) Submission - _____

Points	Advantages
You [____] x [____]	You [____] x [____]

NOTES: _____

_____

_____

_____

MATCH #6

( ) Win ( ) Loss   Final Time:_____
( ) Submission - _____

Points	Advantages
You [____] x [____]	You [____] x [____]

NOTES: _____

_____

_____

_____

Tournament:_____ Date:___/___/___
City: _____ State: ____ Number of Opponents: _____
Age:_____ Rank:_____ Weight:_____
Result:_____ ( ) Gi ( ) No-Gi

MATCH #1
( ) Win ( ) Loss   Final Time:_____
( ) Submission - _____
               Points   **Advantages**
        You [____] x [____]   You [____] x [____]

NOTES: _____
_____
_____
_____

MATCH #2
( ) Win ( ) Loss   Final Time:_____
( ) Submission - _____
               Points   **Advantages**
        You [____] x [____]   You [____] x [____]

NOTES: _____
_____
_____
_____

MATCH #3
( ) Win ( ) Loss   Final Time:_____
( ) Submission - _____
               Points   **Advantages**
        You [____] x [____]   You [____] x [____]

NOTES: _____
_____
_____
_____

MATCH #4

( ) Win ( ) Loss   Final Time:_____

( ) Submission - _____

| Points | Advantages |
You [_____] x [_____]   You [_____] x [_____]

NOTES: _____

_____

_____

_____

MATCH #5

( ) Win ( ) Loss   Final Time:_____

( ) Submission - _____

| Points | Advantages |
You [_____] x [_____]   You [_____] x [_____]

NOTES: _____

_____

_____

_____

MATCH #6

( ) Win ( ) Loss   Final Time:_____

( ) Submission - _____

| Points | Advantages |
You [_____] x [_____]   You [_____] x [_____]

NOTES: _____

_____

_____

_____

Tournament:_____ Date:___/___/___
City: _____ State: ____ Number of Opponents: ____
Age:_____ Rank:_____ Weight:_____
Result:_____ ( ) Gi ( ) No-Gi

MATCH #1
( ) Win ( ) Loss   Final Time:_____
( ) Submission - _____
            Points   **Advantages**
        You [____] x [____]   You [____] x [____]

NOTES: _____

_____

_____

_____

MATCH #2
( ) Win ( ) Loss   Final Time:_____
( ) Submission - _____
            Points   **Advantages**
        You [____] x [____]   You [____] x [____]

NOTES: _____

_____

_____

_____

MATCH #3
( ) Win ( ) Loss   Final Time:_____
( ) Submission - _____
            Points   **Advantages**
        You [____] x [____]   You [____] x [____]

NOTES: _____

_____

_____

_____

MATCH #4

( ) Win   ( ) Loss   Final Time:_____

( ) Submission - _____

| Points | Advantages |
| You [____] x [____] | You [____] x [____] |

NOTES: _____

_____

_____

_____

MATCH #5

( ) Win   ( ) Loss   Final Time:_____

( ) Submission - _____

| Points | Advantages |
| You [____] x [____] | You [____] x [____] |

NOTES: _____

_____

_____

_____

MATCH #6

( ) Win   ( ) Loss   Final Time:_____

( ) Submission - _____

| Points | Advantages |
| You [____] x [____] | You [____] x [____] |

NOTES: _____

_____

_____

_____

Tournament:_____ Date:___/___/___
City: _____ State: ____ Number of Opponents: ____
Age:_____ Rank:_____ Weight:_____
Result:_____ ( ) Gi ( ) No-Gi

MATCH #1

( ) Win ( ) Loss   Final Time:_____
( ) Submission - _____

| | **Points** | | | **Advantages** | |
You [____] x [____]   You [____] x [____]

NOTES: _____

_____
_____
_____

MATCH #2

( ) Win ( ) Loss   Final Time:_____
( ) Submission - _____

Points   **Advantages**
You [____] x [____]   You [____] x [____]

NOTES: _____

_____
_____
_____

MATCH #3

( ) Win ( ) Loss   Final Time:_____
( ) Submission - _____

Points   **Advantages**
You [____] x [____]   You [____] x [____]

NOTES: _____

_____
_____
_____

MATCH #4

( ) Win ( ) Loss   Final Time:_____

( ) Submission - _____

Points	**Advantages**
You [_____] x [_____]	You [_____] x [_____]

NOTES: _____

_____

_____

_____

MATCH #5

( ) Win ( ) Loss   Final Time:_____

( ) Submission - _____

Points	**Advantages**
You [_____] x [_____]	You [_____] x [_____]

NOTES: _____

_____

_____

_____

MATCH #6

( ) Win ( ) Loss   Final Time:_____

( ) Submission - _____

Points	**Advantages**
You [_____] x [_____]	You [_____] x [_____]

NOTES: _____

_____

_____

_____

Tournament:_____ Date:____/____/____

City: _____ State: _____ Number of Opponents: _____

Age:_____ Rank:_____ Weight:_____

Result:_____ ( ) Gi ( ) No-Gi

MATCH #1

( ) Win ( ) Loss   Final Time:_____

( ) Submission - _____

	Points		**Advantages**

You [____] x [____]   You [____] x [____]

NOTES: _____

_____

_____

_____

MATCH #2

( ) Win ( ) Loss   Final Time:_____

( ) Submission - _____

	Points		**Advantages**

You [____] x [____]   You [____] x [____]

NOTES: _____

_____

_____

_____

MATCH #3

( ) Win ( ) Loss   Final Time:_____

( ) Submission - _____

	Points		**Advantages**

You [____] x [____]   You [____] x [____]

NOTES: _____

_____

_____

_____

MATCH #4

( ) Win   ( ) Loss   Final Time:_____
( ) Submission - _____

| **Points** | **Advantages** |
| You [____] x [____] | You [____] x [____] |

NOTES: _____

_____
_____
_____

MATCH #5

( ) Win   ( ) Loss   Final Time:_____
( ) Submission - _____

| **Points** | **Advantages** |
| You [____] x [____] | You [____] x [____] |

NOTES: _____

_____
_____
_____

MATCH #6

( ) Win   ( ) Loss   Final Time:_____
( ) Submission - _____

| **Points** | **Advantages** |
| You [____] x [____] | You [____] x [____] |

NOTES: _____

_____
_____
_____

Tournament:_____ Date:___/___/___
City: _____ State: ____ Number of Opponents: ____
Age:_____ Rank:_____ Weight:_____
Result:_____ ( ) Gi ( ) No-Gi

MATCH #1
( ) Win ( ) Loss   Final Time:_____
( ) Submission - _____
          Points   **Advantages**
    You [____] x [____]   You [____] x [____]

NOTES: _____
_____
_____
_____

MATCH #2
( ) Win ( ) Loss   Final Time:_____
( ) Submission - _____
          Points   **Advantages**
    You [____] x [____]   You [____] x [____]

NOTES: _____
_____
_____
_____

MATCH #3
( ) Win ( ) Loss   Final Time:_____
( ) Submission - _____
          Points   **Advantages**
    You [____] x [____]   You [____] x [____]

NOTES: _____
_____
_____
_____

MATCH #4

( ) Win ( ) Loss   Final Time:_____

( ) Submission - _____

| **Points** | **Advantages** |
| You [____] x [____] | You [____] x [____] |

NOTES: _____

_____

_____

_____

MATCH #5

( ) Win ( ) Loss   Final Time:_____

( ) Submission - _____

| **Points** | **Advantages** |
| You [____] x [____] | You [____] x [____] |

NOTES: _____

_____

_____

_____

MATCH #6

( ) Win ( ) Loss   Final Time:_____

( ) Submission - _____

| **Points** | **Advantages** |
| You [____] x [____] | You [____] x [____] |

NOTES: _____

_____

_____

_____

Tournament:_____ Date:____/____/____
City: _____ State: _____ Number of Opponents: _____
Age:_____ Rank:_____ Weight:_____
Result:_____ ( ) Gi ( ) No-Gi

MATCH #1
( ) Win ( ) Loss   Final Time:_____
( ) Submission - _____
              Points   **Advantages**
     You [____] x [____]   You [____] x [____]

NOTES: _____
_____
_____
_____

MATCH #2
( ) Win ( ) Loss   Final Time:_____
( ) Submission - _____
              Points   **Advantages**
     You [____] x [____]   You [____] x [____]

NOTES: _____
_____
_____
_____

MATCH #3
( ) Win ( ) Loss   Final Time:_____
( ) Submission - _____
              Points   **Advantages**
     You [____] x [____]   You [____] x [____]

NOTES: _____
_____
_____
_____

MATCH #4

( ) Win ( ) Loss   Final Time:_____
( ) Submission - _____

Points   **Advantages**

You [_____] x [_____]   You [_____] x [_____]

NOTES: _____

_____

_____

_____

MATCH #5

( ) Win ( ) Loss   Final Time:_____
( ) Submission - _____

Points   **Advantages**

You [_____] x [_____]   You [_____] x [_____]

NOTES: _____

_____

_____

_____

MATCH #6

( ) Win ( ) Loss   Final Time:_____
( ) Submission - _____

Points   **Advantages**

You [_____] x [_____]   You [_____] x [_____]

NOTES: _____

_____

_____

_____

Tournament:_____ Date:___/___/___
City:_____ State:____ Number of Opponents:____
Age:_____ Rank:_____ Weight:_____
Result:_____ ( ) Gi ( ) No-Gi

MATCH #1

( ) Win ( ) Loss   Final Time:_____
( ) Submission - _____

Points	Advantages
You [____] x [____]	You [____] x [____]

NOTES: _____

_____

_____

_____

MATCH #2

( ) Win ( ) Loss   Final Time:_____
( ) Submission - _____

Points	Advantages
You [____] x [____]	You [____] x [____]

NOTES: _____

_____

_____

_____

MATCH #3

( ) Win ( ) Loss   Final Time:_____
( ) Submission - _____

Points	Advantages
You [____] x [____]	You [____] x [____]

NOTES: _____

_____

_____

_____

MATCH #4

( ) Win ( ) Loss   Final Time:_____
( ) Submission - _____

       Points   **Advantages**
    You [____] x [____]   You [____] x [____]

NOTES: _____

_____

_____

_____

MATCH #5

( ) Win ( ) Loss   Final Time:_____
( ) Submission - _____

       Points   **Advantages**
    You [____] x [____]   You [____] x [____]

NOTES: _____

_____

_____

_____

MATCH #6

( ) Win ( ) Loss   Final Time:_____
( ) Submission - _____

       Points   **Advantages**
    You [____] x [____]   You [____] x [____]

NOTES: _____

_____

_____

_____

BJJ NOTEBOOK

Tournament:_____ Date:___/___/___
City:_____ State:____ Number of Opponents:____
Age:_____ Rank:_____ Weight:_____
Result:_____ ( ) Gi ( ) No-Gi

MATCH #1

( ) Win ( ) Loss   Final Time:_____
( ) Submission - _____

Points	Advantages
You [____] x [____]	You [____] x [____]

NOTES: _____
_____
_____
_____

MATCH #2

( ) Win ( ) Loss   Final Time:_____
( ) Submission - _____

Points	Advantages
You [____] x [____]	You [____] x [____]

NOTES: _____
_____
_____
_____

MATCH #3

( ) Win ( ) Loss   Final Time:_____
( ) Submission - _____

Points	Advantages
You [____] x [____]	You [____] x [____]

NOTES: _____
_____
_____
_____

MATCH #4

( ) Win ( ) Loss   Final Time:_____
( ) Submission - _____

Points	Advantages
You [____] x [____]	You [____] x [____]

NOTES: _____
_____
_____
_____

MATCH #5

( ) Win ( ) Loss   Final Time:_____
( ) Submission - _____

Points	Advantages
You [____] x [____]	You [____] x [____]

NOTES: _____
_____
_____
_____

MATCH #6

( ) Win ( ) Loss   Final Time:_____
( ) Submission - _____

Points	Advantages
You [____] x [____]	You [____] x [____]

NOTES: _____
_____
_____
_____

Tournament:_____ Date:____/____/____
City:_____ State:_____ Number of Opponents:_____
Age:_____ Rank:_____ Weight:_____
Result:_____ ( ) Gi ( ) No-Gi

MATCH #1
( ) Win ( ) Loss   Final Time:_____
( ) Submission - _____

Points	**Advantages**
You [_____] x [_____]	You [_____] x [_____]

NOTES: _____
_____
_____
_____

MATCH #2
( ) Win ( ) Loss   Final Time:_____
( ) Submission - _____

Points	**Advantages**
You [_____] x [_____]	You [_____] x [_____]

NOTES: _____
_____
_____
_____

MATCH #3
( ) Win ( ) Loss   Final Time:_____
( ) Submission - _____

Points	**Advantages**
You [_____] x [_____]	You [_____] x [_____]

NOTES: _____
_____
_____
_____

MATCH #4

( ) Win ( ) Loss   Final Time:_____
( ) Submission - _____

	Points	**Advantages**
	You [___] x [___]	You [___] x [___]

NOTES: _____

_____

_____

_____

MATCH #5

( ) Win ( ) Loss   Final Time:_____
( ) Submission - _____

	Points	**Advantages**
	You [___] x [___]	You [___] x [___]

NOTES: _____

_____

_____

_____

MATCH #6

( ) Win ( ) Loss   Final Time:_____
( ) Submission - _____

	Points	**Advantages**
	You [___] x [___]	You [___] x [___]

NOTES: _____

_____

_____

_____

BJJ NOTEBOOK

Tournament:_____ Date:____/____/____
City:_____ State:_____ Number of Opponents:_____
Age:_____ Rank:_____ Weight:_____
Result:_____ ( ) Gi ( ) No-Gi

MATCH #1
( ) Win ( ) Loss   Final Time:_____
( ) Submission - _____
           Points   **Advantages**
      You [____] x [____]   You [____] x [____]

NOTES: _____
_____
_____
_____

MATCH #2
( ) Win ( ) Loss   Final Time:_____
( ) Submission - _____
           Points   **Advantages**
      You [____] x [____]   You [____] x [____]

NOTES: _____
_____
_____
_____

MATCH #3
( ) Win ( ) Loss   Final Time:_____
( ) Submission - _____
           Points   **Advantages**
      You [____] x [____]   You [____] x [____]

NOTES: _____
_____
_____
_____

MATCH #4

( ) Win   ( ) Loss   Final Time:_____
( ) Submission - _____

	Points	**Advantages**
You [____] x [____]	You [____] x [____]

NOTES: _____

_____
_____
_____

MATCH #5

( ) Win   ( ) Loss   Final Time:_____
( ) Submission - _____

	Points	**Advantages**
You [____] x [____]	You [____] x [____]

NOTES: _____

_____
_____
_____

MATCH #6

( ) Win   ( ) Loss   Final Time:_____
( ) Submission - _____

	Points	**Advantages**
You [____] x [____]	You [____] x [____]

NOTES: _____

_____
_____
_____

Tournament:_____ Date:___/___/___
City:_____ State:____ Number of Opponents:____
Age:_____ Rank:_____ Weight:_____
Result:_____ ( ) Gi ( ) No-Gi

MATCH #1
( ) Win ( ) Loss   Final Time:_____
( ) Submission - _____

Points	Advantages
You [____] x [____]	You [____] x [____]

NOTES: _____
_____
_____
_____

MATCH #2
( ) Win ( ) Loss   Final Time:_____
( ) Submission - _____

Points	Advantages
You [____] x [____]	You [____] x [____]

NOTES: _____
_____
_____
_____

MATCH #3
( ) Win ( ) Loss   Final Time:_____
( ) Submission - _____

Points	Advantages
You [____] x [____]	You [____] x [____]

NOTES: _____
_____
_____
_____

MATCH #4

( ) Win ( ) Loss   Final Time:_____
( ) Submission - _____

Points	**Advantages**
You [____] x [____]	You [____] x [____]

NOTES: _____
_____
_____
_____

MATCH #5

( ) Win ( ) Loss   Final Time:_____
( ) Submission - _____

Points	**Advantages**
You [____] x [____]	You [____] x [____]

NOTES: _____
_____
_____
_____

MATCH #6

( ) Win ( ) Loss   Final Time:_____
( ) Submission - _____

Points	**Advantages**
You [____] x [____]	You [____] x [____]

NOTES: _____
_____
_____
_____

Tournament:_____ Date:___/___/___
City:_____ State:____ Number of Opponents:____
Age:_____ Rank:_____ Weight:_____
Result:_____ ( ) Gi ( ) No-Gi

MATCH #1
( ) Win ( ) Loss   Final Time:_____
( ) Submission - _____
          Points   **Advantages**
     You [____] x [____]   You [____] x [____]

NOTES: _____
_____
_____
_____

MATCH #2
( ) Win ( ) Loss   Final Time:_____
( ) Submission - _____
          Points   **Advantages**
     You [____] x [____]   You [____] x [____]

NOTES: _____
_____
_____
_____

MATCH #3
( ) Win ( ) Loss   Final Time:_____
( ) Submission - _____
          Points   **Advantages**
     You [____] x [____]   You [____] x [____]

NOTES: _____
_____
_____
_____

MATCH #4

( ) Win ( ) Loss   Final Time:_____
( ) Submission - _____

       Points   **Advantages**

    You [____] x [____]   You [____] x [____]

NOTES: _____

_____

_____

_____

MATCH #5

( ) Win ( ) Loss   Final Time:_____
( ) Submission - _____

       Points   **Advantages**

    You [____] x [____]   You [____] x [____]

NOTES: _____

_____

_____

_____

MATCH #6

( ) Win ( ) Loss   Final Time:_____
( ) Submission - _____

       Points   **Advantages**

    You [____] x [____]   You [____] x [____]

NOTES: _____

_____

_____

_____

Tournament:_____ Date:___/___/___
City: _____ State: ____ Number of Opponents: ____
Age:_____ Rank:_____ Weight:_____
Result:_____ ( ) Gi ( ) No-Gi

MATCH #1
( ) Win ( ) Loss   Final Time:_____
( ) Submission - _____
       Points   **Advantages**
    You [____] x [____]   You [____] x [____]

NOTES: _____

_____

_____

_____

MATCH #2
( ) Win ( ) Loss   Final Time:_____
( ) Submission - _____
       Points   **Advantages**
    You [____] x [____]   You [____] x [____]

NOTES: _____

_____

_____

_____

MATCH #3
( ) Win ( ) Loss   Final Time:_____
( ) Submission - _____
       Points   **Advantages**
    You [____] x [____]   You [____] x [____]

NOTES: _____

_____

_____

_____

MATCH #4

( ) Win ( ) Loss   Final Time:_____

( ) Submission - _____

	Points		**Advantages**
You [____] x [____]		You [____] x [____]	

NOTES: _____

_____

_____

_____

MATCH #5

( ) Win ( ) Loss   Final Time:_____

( ) Submission - _____

	Points		**Advantages**
You [____] x [____]		You [____] x [____]	

NOTES: _____

_____

_____

_____

MATCH #6

( ) Win ( ) Loss   Final Time:_____

( ) Submission - _____

	Points		**Advantages**
You [____] x [____]		You [____] x [____]	

NOTES: _____

_____

_____

_____

Tournament:_____ Date:____/____/____
City: _____ State: ____ Number of Opponents: ____
Age:_____ Rank:_____ Weight:_____
Result:_____ ( ) Gi ( ) No-Gi

MATCH #1

( ) Win ( ) Loss   Final Time:_____
( ) Submission - _____
        Points   **Advantages**
    You [____] x [____]   You [____] x [____]

NOTES: _____
_____
_____
_____

MATCH #2

( ) Win ( ) Loss   Final Time:_____
( ) Submission - _____
        Points   **Advantages**
    You [____] x [____]   You [____] x [____]

NOTES: _____
_____
_____
_____

MATCH #3

( ) Win ( ) Loss   Final Time:_____
( ) Submission - _____
        Points   **Advantages**
    You [____] x [____]   You [____] x [____]

NOTES: _____
_____
_____
_____

MATCH #4

( ) Win ( ) Loss   Final Time:_____
( ) Submission - _____

Points	**Advantages**
You [____] x [____]	You [____] x [____]

NOTES: _____

_____

_____

_____

MATCH #5

( ) Win ( ) Loss   Final Time:_____
( ) Submission - _____

Points	**Advantages**
You [____] x [____]	You [____] x [____]

NOTES: _____

_____

_____

_____

MATCH #6

( ) Win ( ) Loss   Final Time:_____
( ) Submission - _____

Points	**Advantages**
You [____] x [____]	You [____] x [____]

NOTES: _____

_____

_____

_____

BJJ NOTEBOOK

Tournament:_____ Date:____/____/____
City: _____ State: _____ Number of Opponents: _____
Age:_____ Rank:_____ Weight:_____
Result:_____ ( ) Gi ( ) No-Gi

MATCH #1

( ) Win ( ) Loss   Final Time:_____
( ) Submission - _____

Points	Advantages
You [____] x [____]	You [____] x [____]

NOTES: _____

_____

_____

_____

MATCH #2

( ) Win ( ) Loss   Final Time:_____
( ) Submission - _____

Points	Advantages
You [____] x [____]	You [____] x [____]

NOTES: _____

_____

_____

_____

MATCH #3

( ) Win ( ) Loss   Final Time:_____
( ) Submission - _____

Points	Advantages
You [____] x [____]	You [____] x [____]

NOTES: _____

_____

_____

_____

MATCH #4

( ) Win ( ) Loss   Final Time:_____

( ) Submission - _____

          Points   **Advantages**

    You [____] x [____]   You [____] x [____]

NOTES: _____

_____

_____

_____

MATCH #5

( ) Win ( ) Loss   Final Time:_____

( ) Submission - _____

          Points   **Advantages**

    You [____] x [____]   You [____] x [____]

NOTES: _____

_____

_____

_____

MATCH #6

( ) Win ( ) Loss   Final Time:_____

( ) Submission - _____

          Points   **Advantages**

    You [____] x [____]   You [____] x [____]

NOTES: _____

_____

_____

_____

Tournament:_____ Date:____/____/____
City: _____ State: _____ Number of Opponents: _____
Age:_____ Rank:_____ Weight:_____
Result:_____ ( ) Gi ( ) No-Gi

MATCH #1
( ) Win ( ) Loss   Final Time:_____
( ) Submission - _____
              Points   **Advantages**
      You [____] x [____]   You [____] x [____]

NOTES: _____
_____
_____
_____

MATCH #2
( ) Win ( ) Loss   Final Time:_____
( ) Submission - _____
              Points   **Advantages**
      You [____] x [____]   You [____] x [____]

NOTES: _____
_____
_____
_____

MATCH #3
( ) Win ( ) Loss   Final Time:_____
( ) Submission - _____
              Points   **Advantages**
      You [____] x [____]   You [____] x [____]

NOTES: _____
_____
_____
_____

MATCH #4

( ) Win ( ) Loss   Final Time:_____
( ) Submission - _____

| Points | Advantages |
| You [_____] x [_____] | You [_____] x [_____] |

NOTES: _____

_____
_____
_____

MATCH #5

( ) Win ( ) Loss   Final Time:_____
( ) Submission - _____

| Points | Advantages |
| You [_____] x [_____] | You [_____] x [_____] |

NOTES: _____

_____
_____
_____

MATCH #6

( ) Win ( ) Loss   Final Time:_____
( ) Submission - _____

| Points | Advantages |
| You [_____] x [_____] | You [_____] x [_____] |

NOTES: _____

_____
_____
_____

BJJ NOTEBOOK

Tournament:_____ Date:____/____/____
City:_____ State:____ Number of Opponents:_____
Age:_____ Rank:_____ Weight:_____
Result:_____ ( ) Gi ( ) No-Gi

MATCH #1
( ) Win ( ) Loss   Final Time:_____
( ) Submission - _____

	Points		Advantages
You [____] x [____]		You [____] x [____]	

NOTES: _____
_____
_____
_____

MATCH #2
( ) Win ( ) Loss   Final Time:_____
( ) Submission - _____

	Points		Advantages
You [____] x [____]		You [____] x [____]	

NOTES: _____
_____
_____
_____

MATCH #3
( ) Win ( ) Loss   Final Time:_____
( ) Submission - _____

	Points		Advantages
You [____] x [____]		You [____] x [____]	

NOTES: _____
_____
_____
_____

MATCH #4

( ) Win ( ) Loss   Final Time:_____
( ) Submission - _____

Points	Advantages
You [_____] x [_____]	You [_____] x [_____]

NOTES: _____

_____

_____

_____

MATCH #5

( ) Win ( ) Loss   Final Time:_____
( ) Submission - _____

Points	Advantages
You [_____] x [_____]	You [_____] x [_____]

NOTES: _____

_____

_____

_____

MATCH #6

( ) Win ( ) Loss   Final Time:_____
( ) Submission - _____

Points	Advantages
You [_____] x [_____]	You [_____] x [_____]

NOTES: _____

_____

_____

_____

BJJ NOTEBOOK
MATCH RECORD
(Check each time you won or loss a match and how)

WINS: □ □ □ □ □ □ □ □ □ □ □ □ □ □ □ □ □ □
□ □ □ □ □ □ □ □ □ □ □ □ □ □ □ □ □ □
□ □ □ □ □ □ □ □ □ □ □ □ □ □ □ □ □ □

By Submission: □ □ □ □ □ □ □ □ □ □ □ □ □ □ □
□ □ □ □ □ □ □ □ □ □ □ □ □ □ □

By Points: □ □ □ □ □ □ □ □ □ □ □ □ □ □ □
□ □ □ □ □ □ □ □ □ □ □ □ □ □ □

By Advantage: □ □ □ □ □ □ □ □ □ □ □ □ □ □ □
□ □ □ □ □ □ □ □ □ □ □ □ □ □ □

Injury: □ □ □ □ □   Disqualification: □ □ □ □ □

LOSSES: □ □ □ □ □ □ □ □ □ □ □ □ □ □ □ □ □ □
□ □ □ □ □ □ □ □ □ □ □ □ □ □ □ □ □ □
□ □ □ □ □ □ □ □ □ □ □ □ □ □ □ □ □ □

By Submission: □ □ □ □ □ □ □ □ □ □ □ □ □ □ □
□ □ □ □ □ □ □ □ □ □ □ □ □ □ □

By Points: □ □ □ □ □ □ □ □ □ □ □ □ □ □ □
□ □ □ □ □ □ □ □ □ □ □ □ □ □ □

By Advantage: □ □ □ □ □ □ □ □ □ □ □ □ □ □ □
□ □ □ □ □ □ □ □ □ □ □ □ □ □ □

Injury: □ □ □ □ □   Disqualification: □ □ □ □ □

WINS BY SUBMISSION
(Check each time you won by any submission)

Armbar.........................: □ □ □ □ □ □ □ □ □ □ □ □ □ □

Keylock........................: □ □ □ □ □ □ □ □ □ □ □ □ □ □

Kimura.........................: □ □ □ □ □ □ □ □ □ □ □ □ □ □

Omoplata......................: □ □ □ □ □ □ □ □ □ □ □ □ □ □

Wrist lock.....................: □ □ □ □ □ □ □ □ □ □ □ □ □ □

Leg lock.......................: □ □ □ □ □ □ □ □ □ □ □ □ □ □

Foot lock......................: □ □ □ □ □ □ □ □ □ □ □ □ □ □

_____ : □ □ □ □ □ □ □ □ □ □ □ □ □ □

_____ : □ □ □ □ □ □ □ □ □ □ □ □ □ □

_____ : □ □ □ □ □ □ □ □ □ □ □ □ □ □

_____ : □ □ □ □ □ □ □ □ □ □ □ □ □ □

_____ : □ □ □ □ □ □ □ □ □ □ □ □ □ □

Triangle.......................: □ □ □ □ □ □ □ □ □ □ □ □ □ □

Arm triangle.................: □ □ □ □ □ □ □ □ □ □ □ □ □ □

Guillotine.....................: □ □ □ □ □ □ □ □ □ □ □ □ □ □

Frontal gi choke.............: □ □ □ □ □ □ □ □ □ □ □ □ □ □

Rear gi choke................: □ □ □ □ □ □ □ □ □ □ □ □ □ □

Lateral gi choke.............: □ □ □ □ □ □ □ □ □ □ □ □ □ □

Rear naked choke..........: □ □ □ □ □ □ □ □ □ □ □ □ □ □

_____ : □ □ □ □ □ □ □ □ □ □ □ □ □ □

_____ : □ □ □ □ □ □ □ □ □ □ □ □ □ □

_____ : □ □ □ □ □ □ □ □ □ □ □ □ □ □

_____ : □ □ □ □ □ □ □ □ □ □ □ □ □ □

_____ : □ □ □ □ □ □ □ □ □ □ □ □ □ □

LOSSES BY SUBMISSION
(Check each time you were submitted by any submission)

Armbar..................... : □ □ □ □ □ □ □ □ □ □ □ □ □ □

Keylock.................. : □ □ □ □ □ □ □ □ □ □ □ □ □ □

Kimura.................... : □ □ □ □ □ □ □ □ □ □ □ □ □ □

Omoplata.................. : □ □ □ □ □ □ □ □ □ □ □ □ □ □

Wrist lock................. : □ □ □ □ □ □ □ □ □ □ □ □ □ □

Leg lock.................. : □ □ □ □ □ □ □ □ □ □ □ □ □ □

Foot lock................... : □ □ □ □ □ □ □ □ □ □ □ □ □ □

_____ : □ □ □ □ □ □ □ □ □ □ □ □ □ □

_____ : □ □ □ □ □ □ □ □ □ □ □ □ □ □

_____ : □ □ □ □ □ □ □ □ □ □ □ □ □ □

_____ : □ □ □ □ □ □ □ □ □ □ □ □ □ □

_____ : □ □ □ □ □ □ □ □ □ □ □ □ □ □

Triangle................... : □ □ □ □ □ □ □ □ □ □ □ □ □ □

Arm triangle............... : □ □ □ □ □ □ □ □ □ □ □ □ □ □

Guillotine.................. : □ □ □ □ □ □ □ □ □ □ □ □ □ □

Frontal gi choke............ : □ □ □ □ □ □ □ □ □ □ □ □ □ □

Rear gi choke.............. : □ □ □ □ □ □ □ □ □ □ □ □ □ □

Lateral gi choke............ : □ □ □ □ □ □ □ □ □ □ □ □ □ □

Rear naked choke.......... : □ □ □ □ □ □ □ □ □ □ □ □ □ □

_____ : □ □ □ □ □ □ □ □ □ □ □ □ □ □

_____ : □ □ □ □ □ □ □ □ □ □ □ □ □ □

_____ : □ □ □ □ □ □ □ □ □ □ □ □ □ □

_____ : □ □ □ □ □ □ □ □ □ □ □ □ □ □

_____ : □ □ □ □ □ □ □ □ □ □ □ □ □ □

POINTS TRACKING
(Write down in each field the total amount of points scored in a match)

My Points Per Match

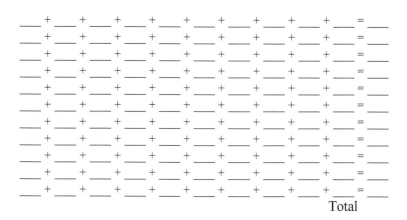

Total

Adversary Points Per Match

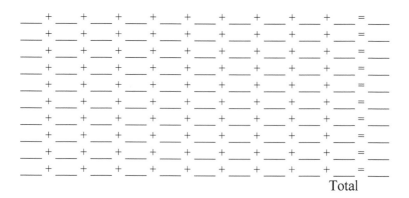

Total

BJJ NOTEBOOK
ADVANTAGES TRACKING
(Write down in each field the total amount of advantages scored in a match)

My Advantages Per Match

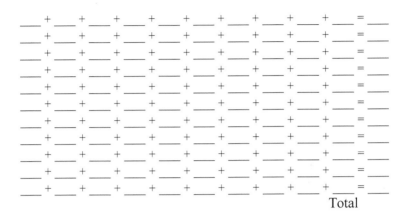

Total

Adversary Advantages Per Match

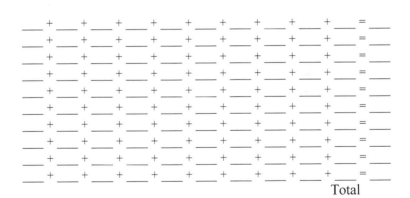

Total

TOURNAMENT RESULTS

Tournament Name: _____

Date: ___/___/___ Rank: _____ Age: _____ Weight: _____
Location: _____ Result: _____

Tournament Name: _____

Date: ___/___/___ Rank: _____ Age: _____ Weight: _____
Location: _____ Result: _____

Tournament Name: _____

Date: ___/___/___ Rank: _____ Age: _____ Weight: _____
Location: _____ Result: _____

Tournament Name: _____

Date: ___/___/___ Rank: _____ Age: _____ Weight: _____
Location: _____ Result: _____

Tournament Name: _____

Date: ___/___/___ Rank: _____ Age: _____ Weight: _____
Location: _____ Result: _____

Tournament Name: _____

Date: ___/___/___ Rank: _____ Age: _____ Weight: _____
Location: _____ Result: _____

Tournament Name: _____

Date: ___/___/___ Rank: _____ Age: _____ Weight: _____
Location: _____ Result: _____

Tournament Name: _____

Date: ___/___/___ Rank: _____ Age: _____ Weight: _____
Location: _____ Result: _____

Tournament Name: _____

Date: ___/___/___ Rank: _____ Age: _____ Weight: _____
Location: _____ Result: _____

BJJ NOTEBOOK

Tournament Name: _____

Date: ___/___/___ Rank: _____ Age: _____ Weight: _____

Location: _____ Result: _____

Tournament Name: _____

Date: ___/___/___ Rank: _____ Age: _____ Weight: _____

Location: _____ Result: _____

Tournament Name: _____

Date: ___/___/___ Rank: _____ Age: _____ Weight: _____

Location: _____ Result: _____

Tournament Name: _____

Date: ___/___/___ Rank: _____ Age: _____ Weight: _____

Location: _____ Result: _____

Tournament Name: _____

Date: ___/___/___ Rank: _____ Age: _____ Weight: _____

Location: _____ Result: _____

Tournament Name: _____

Date: ___/___/___ Rank: _____ Age: _____ Weight: _____

Location: _____ Result: _____

Tournament Name: _____

Date: ___/___/___ Rank: _____ Age: _____ Weight: _____

Location: _____ Result: _____

Tournament Name: _____

Date: ___/___/___ Rank: _____ Age: _____ Weight: _____

Location: _____ Result: _____

Tournament Name: _____

Date: ___/___/___ Rank: _____ Age: _____ Weight: _____

Location: _____ Result: _____

15 INJURY LOG

It is probably safe to say that BJJ athletes put their bodies through more stress and trauma than most people. Training is year-round and some trainers attend weekend tournaments where competitors are eager to win and perform at 100% of their capabilities. During regular practices, students work on conditioning, strengthening drills, skill training, and sparring. The season never ends in BJJ.

During these strenuous exercises and competitions injuries are inevitable. However, many athletes elect not to address these issues during the year. They feel if they report injuries they will be taken off the mats and not be cleared to train. Often, athletes continue to train despite injuries, or use pain reducing or numbing agents to combat and temporarily relieve the pain. The inherent flaw in this tactic is that although the athlete can not feel it, they are most likely exacerbating the injury by continued stress on the affected area. Injury can be minimized by doing an effective warm up, which consists of a heart raiser to get your pulse up, followed by specific and dynamic stretches. Strengthening muscles, increasing flexibility, taking breaks, using proper techniques, sparing safely, staying hydrated and stopping the activity if there is pain are the best tips that you can follow to have a safe BJJ journey.

When injured always try to watch missed classes. Your instructor may be showing a new technique or an additional detail that you will benefit from seeing.

Use the following pages to record injuries. It will allow you to make sure you are training correctly as you can track re-occurring injuries and follow-up with treatments.

Date of Injury: ____/____/____   Days Off: _____

Description of Injury: _____

_____

How did it happen? _____

_____

_____

Treatment plan: _____

_____

_____

Date of Injury: ____/____/____   Days Off: _____

Description of Injury: _____

_____

How did it happen? _____

_____

_____

Treatment plan: _____

_____

_____

Date of Injury: ___/___/___   Days Off: _____

Description of Injury: _____

_____

How did it happen? _____

_____

_____

Treatment plan: _____

_____

_____

Date of Injury: ___/___/___   Days Off: _____

Description of Injury: _____

_____

How did it happen? _____

_____

_____

Treatment plan: _____

_____

_____

BJJ NOTEBOOK

Date of Injury: ____/____/____   Days Off: _____

Description of Injury: _____

_____

How did it happen? _____

_____

_____

Treatment plan: _____

_____

_____

Date of Injury: ____/____/____   Days Off: _____

Description of Injury: _____

_____

How did it happen? _____

_____

_____

Treatment plan: _____

_____

_____

Date of Injury: ____/____/____   Days Off: _____

Description of Injury: _____

_____

How did it happen? _____

_____

_____

Treatment plan: _____

_____

_____

Date of Injury: ____/____/____   Days Off: _____

Description of Injury: _____

_____

How did it happen? _____

_____

_____

Treatment plan: _____

_____

_____

Date of Injury: ____/____/____   Days Off: _____

Description of Injury: _____

_____

How did it happen? _____

_____

_____

Treatment plan: _____

_____

_____

Date of Injury: ____/____/____   Days Off: _____

Description of Injury: _____

_____

How did it happen? _____

_____

_____

Treatment plan: _____

_____

_____

16 PHOTO GALLERY

Use this section to save and record important moments you will live throughout your BJJ journey. A group photo with your current training partners, a tournament, a podium photo, a BJJ trip, a funny moment, a belt promotion, you name it! There will be plenty of priceless moments to come!

11465428R00129

Printed in Great Britain
by Amazon.co.uk, Ltd.,
Marston Gate.